Insights on the Business Climate in Uzbekistan

OECD
BETTER POLICIES FOR BETTER LIVES

This work is published under the responsibility of the Secretary-General of the OECD. The opinions expressed and arguments employed herein do not necessarily reflect the official views of the Member countries of the OECD.

This document, as well as any data and map included herein, are without prejudice to the status of or sovereignty over any territory, to the delimitation of international frontiers and boundaries and to the name of any territory, city or area.

The statistical data for Israel are supplied by and under the responsibility of the relevant Israeli authorities. The use of such data by the OECD is without prejudice to the status of the Golan Heights, East Jerusalem and Israeli settlements in the West Bank under the terms of international law.

Please cite this publication as:
OECD (2023), *Insights on the Business Climate in Uzbekistan*, OECD Publishing, Paris, https://doi.org/10.1787/317ce52e-en.

ISBN 978-92-64-98973-3 (print)
ISBN 978-92-64-85189-4 (pdf)
ISBN 978-92-64-35733-4 (HTML)
ISBN 978-92-64-65114-2 (epub)

Photo credits: Cover © Hairem/Shutterstock.com.

Corrigenda to OECD publications may be found on line at: www.oecd.org/about/publishing/corrigenda.htm.

Foreword

Uzbekistan is the second largest economy in Central Asia, and the government aims to achieve upper-middle income status by 2030. Real GDP grew by 5.3% in 2022, down from 7.4% the previous year. For almost three decades, the country's post-independence growth was driven chiefly by state-directed investment and industrialisation, with international trade and private sector development significantly limited. This has changed since the launch of a wide-ranging programme of reforms in 2017.

Uzbekistan emerged on a relatively strong footing following the COVID-19 crisis, and as of spring 2023 the impact of Russia's war in Ukraine has been muted. The resilience of the country in face of serious recent economic shocks is testament to the prudent and agile policy response of the authorities, as well as the country's position to benefit from higher international prices for key exports such as gold. Nevertheless, the growth outlook is uncertain, with the continuation of Russia's war in Ukraine and the associated potential for further sanctions to affect Uzbekistan's trade, persistently high domestic inflation and tighter global financial conditions all contributing to a challenging short-to-medium term context. Since the reform process began, the government has made considerable efforts to diminish the role of the state in the economy and enable the private sector to play a more expansive role in economic development.

Nevertheless, the resilience of Uzbekistan's economy continues to be hampered by a relatively underdeveloped private sector. Understanding the issues that prevent the private sector from investing, hiring, innovating and growing will be key to ensuring sustainable prosperity in the years ahead. It will also be critical to the success of Uzbekistan in navigating the twin transitions of digitalisation and decarbonisation. This report brings together recent OECD analysis on key business climate issues in the country in order to focus policy attention on the most pressing questions facing the business community in the country.

The content of the report is guided by a survey of international – primarily European – firms operating in Uzbekistan. The survey was an opportunity to gauge business sentiment among a small cohort of international firms of the type that the government is actively seeking to attract to the country. The concerns, observations and positive appraisals gathered through the survey largely dovetail with the OECD's own analysis on business climate issues in Uzbekistan.

Acknowledgements

This report was prepared by the OECD Eurasia Division of the OECD Global Relations and Co-operation Secretariat (GRC), under the guidance of Mr William Tompson, Head of the OECD Eurasia Division, and Mr Grégory Lecomte, Head of the Central Asia Unit. The work was carried out in the context of the OECD Eurasia Competitiveness Programme as part of the OECD Central Asia Initiative. The work was financed by the European Union (EU).

The report was drafted by Mr Luke Mackle, Policy Analyst at the OECD Eurasia Division. The report benefited from substantial statistical and editorial support from Mr Hugo Brisebard, Junior Policy Analyst at the OECD Eurasia Division. The report was enriched with substantive comments from Ms Peline Atamer, Programme Manager, and Ms Amélie Schurich-Rey and Ms Céléste Laporte, Policy Analysts, all of the OECD Eurasia Division. Valuable editorial and publication support was also provided by Ms Elisa Larrakoetxea, and excellent administrative support was provided by Ms Anna Chahtahtinsky, both of the OECD Eurasia Division.

The report draws upon a survey of private firms and private sector organisations in Uzbekistan, and the OECD is indebted to each of the firms and organisations that took the time to respond to the survey. The OECD is also grateful to a number of development partners that provided comments and reflections on the survey and its findings.

The OECD would like to thank colleagues at the Delegation of the European Delegation to Uzbekistan for their support in delivering this report. In particular, the OECD would like to thank Ms Charlotte Adriaen, Ambassador of the EU to the Republic of Uzbekistan, and Mr Wim Riepma, Head of Co-operation, and Mr Elbek Khodjaev, Project Manager, both of the EU Delegation the Republic of Uzbekistan. The OECD would also like to thank Ms Sarah Rinaldi, Head of Unit of the Directorate-General of International Partnerships at the European Commission for her support.

Table of contents

FIGURES

TABLES

Executive summary

Uzbekistan has embarked on a wide-ranging economic reform programme, but much remains to be done

Since embarking on a wide-ranging reform programme in 2017, Uzbekistan has made considerable progress in creating the framework conditions for a competitive private sector. In the first decades of independence, Uzbekistan's growth was primarily driven by a state-led model of industrialisation, state-owned enterprises predominated in most sectors of the economy, and the role of international trade and the private sector significantly limited. Whilst macroeconomic performance was relatively strong, this development model tended to hamper the reallocation of human and fixed capital needed to drive structural transformation. Since the reform process accelerated in 2017, the government has made considerable efforts to reduce the direct role of the state in the economy and enable the private sector to play a more expansive role in economic development.

The steps taken by the government in recent years are contributing to greater socio-economic resilience and opening up the economy to new investment, technology and ideas. Uzbekistan emerged on a relatively strong footing following the COVID-19 crisis, and as of spring 2023, the impact of Russia's war has been muted. The resilience of the country in face of these external shocks is testament to the prudent and agile policy response of the authorities, as well as the country's ability to benefit from higher international prices for key exports such as gold. Rising levels of investment, a resumption of accession talks with the World Trade Organisation, regulatory liberalisation for foreign direct investment (FDI), and reforms across a vast array of policy domains all point to the country moving towards a model of growth that can be more inclusive and resilient.

Uzbekistan nevertheless remains at a relatively early stage of its journey towards an open and competitive market economy, and there remain a number of challenges that continue to inhibit the development of private enterprise. Rather than being the locomotive of economic growth, the government is gradually beginning to refashion its role as an enabler of private sector development and investment, for example, by improving the framework conditions – skills, access to finance, infrastructure, etc. – necessary for entrepreneurship. Rationalising the role of the state in the country's economy and addressing the competition-related imbalances that its historical role may have created, is a key issue that many of the government's policy interventions to support private sector development address.

Ongoing reforms to support entrepreneurship and investment can improve growth and productivity performance

The OECD conducted a private sector survey in Uzbekistan to gauge business sentiment on the government's ongoing reform process and to help identify opportunities and challenges in the business climate. The survey was small but focussed, targeting foreign firms active in Uzbekistan as well as a number of business and trade organisations. Respondents were asked to highlight reform progress and challenges, to identify policy issues they considered priorities for action, to give their views on the impact of Russia's war in Ukraine and the COVID pandemic on doing business in Uzbekistan, and to share their thoughts on policies to support the private sector in the context of the digital and green transitions.

Three major priorities emerge from the survey. First, respondents emphasised the importance of making trade across borders simpler, with only a handful of firms saying that there had been significant progress on trade facilitation in the past five years. While recognising the significant efforts the government has made to improve the regulatory environment for firms, respondents also emphasised the importance of complementary pro-competition policies to ensure that firms could enter freely and compete on a level playing field. Finally, while appreciating the opportunities that digitalisation presented in Uzbekistan, firms noted the need for greater investment in connectivity infrastructure and skills development.

Improving trade facilitation can help firms internationalise and strengthen Uzbekistan's position as a regional trade hub

A significant share of respondents noted the importance of market opportunities – domestic and regional – as a factor in their decisions to enter Uzbekistan. Firms were positive on a number of areas where government action had made international trade easier, particularly exchange rate liberalisation and the relaxation of currency restrictions. Yet, a significant number of firms noted the persistence of logistical bottlenecks and disruptions that made the practicalities of international trade slow and costly. Some of these disruptions were short-term, related to Russia's war in Ukraine and the COVID-19 pandemic, but the survey results suggest a general a lack of enthusiasm for the overall speed of trade facilitation reforms.

Ensuring that market-seeking firms are able to trade easily, and that local SMEs are able to integrate into potential new value chains raises the importance of trade facilitation and export promotion. Uzbekistan has long recognised the importance of reforms to support trade facilitation in making it easier for local SMEs to trade internationally and to compete abroad. While the country's performance in the OECD Trade Facilitation Indicators (TFIs) suggest that Uzbekistan is gradually improving its trade facilitation framework, there remains a significant gap with the OECD average that targeted policy action could help narrow. Additional targeted support to help SMEs access foreign markets and raise their awareness of the demands of these markets could also significantly help internationalise the private sector.

Pro-competition reforms would enhance the benefits of reforms that have opened up the country to investment

Firms generally considered the business climate in Uzbekistan to be friendly, acknowledging clear progress in most of the indicators on which they were surveyed. Respondents were most positive about efforts to ease business registration and licensing. Many of the issues that emerged as most problematic were related to the establishment of a level playing field between public and private firms, with competition policy and enforcement a particular challenge. On each of the sub-indicators for competition policy, a majority reported that it was weak (institutional framework for competition policy – 52%; concentration control – 54%; measures in place against cartels and concerted practices – 57%; control of market dominance and monopoly practices – 67%).

Additional pro-competition reforms can help enable the private sector to thrive in a liberalising regulatory environment for business and investment. Firms' concerns over competition issues are in contrast to the positive appraisal of reform progress in other areas, and these concerns come amidst a large number of institutional changes that have been put in place precisely to level the playing field for private business. That firms have yet to feel the benefits of these legal reforms speaks to implementation challenges, the scope of the legal reforms enacted to date, and a complicated range of adjacent reforms (*e.g.*, in land and other factor markets, or corporatisation and privatisation of state assets) that that are required to level playing the field between public and private enterprise.

New skills and greater investment in connectivity infrastructure and digital technologies are necessary for future economic competitiveness and inclusion

Respondents were enthusiastic about the business opportunities associated with Uzbekistan's digital transformation. A significant majority considered digitalisation to present new opportunities for them in the country, and many had already adopted advanced digital tools such as customer relationship management software and cloud-based computing services. Firms were also positive about the government's efforts to use digitalisation to improve public service delivery. Nevertheless, respondents noted a number of challenges that held back the uptake and use of digital tools at the firm level.

Uzbekistan needs greater investment in connectivity and digital infrastructure, as well as in the skills that firms need to make the most of digital opportunities. While the cost of fixed broadband in Uzbekistan is relatively high, access costs are converging with the OECD average and trending towards the 2% GNI target set out in the Sustainable Development Goals. However, the quality of access is highly variable across the country, while the investment in the information and communication technologies (as a share of total investment) needed to make the most of an expanded connectivity infrastructure remains far below the OECD average. More can also be done to address digital skills needs and to help firms recognise the opportunities digital technologies offer in terms of production and innovation.

Unshackling the private sector can advance Uzbekistan's journey towards a thriving, competitive economy

Uzbekistan has strong fundamentals for long-term, sustainable growth. The country is populous, entrepreneurial and endowed with natural resources, and it has a government committed to an ambitious reform agenda. Its progress since 2017 has been impressive, but to achieve meaningful structural reform, with the private sector playing an expanded role in economic development, it will need to tackle more challenging issues in the years ahead. For many of the areas highlighted in this report, reform implementation will be more difficult than reform design and will demand creativity, new capacities and political will from the government and public agencies. The green and digital transitions add a further set of considerations for the authorities to confront as they proceed with their reform programme, but they also present enormous opportunities for Uzbekistan should the country be successful in unshackling the private sector from the constraints that have stymied entrepreneurship in the past.

1 Introduction

Addressing barriers to private-sector development has been a long-standing ambition of the government of Uzbekistan, with an extensive programme of reforms that began in 2017 redoubling efforts to foster the growth of a more competitive and productive population of private-sector firms. Uzbekistan needs a more dynamic and innovative private sector if it is to meet the challenges and seize the opportunities of the green and digital transitions, which create a new impetus for accelerating these reforms. A survey of the private sector in Uzbekistan provided an opportunity to gather new insights into firm-level perceptions of the ongoing reform process and to refocus the attention of policymakers on some of the most pressing issues.

1.1. Introduction

Uzbekistan is the second largest economy in Central Asia, and the government has ambitions to achieve upper-middle income status by 2030. The country is populous, double-land locked, possesses considerable natural resource wealth, and has an entrepreneurial if constrained private sector. Prior to the beginning of a wide-ranging and ambitious programme of reforms in 2017, the country's growth since independence in 1991 had been primarily driven by state-directed investment and industrialisation, with international trade and private sector development significantly limited. Since the reform process began, the government has made considerable efforts to diminish the role of the state in the economy and enable the private sector to play a more expansive role in economic development.

Uzbekistan emerged on a relatively strong footing following the COVID-19 crisis, and as of spring 2023 the impact of Russia's war in Ukraine has been muted. The economy grew by 5.3% in 2022, down from 7.4% the previous year (World Bank, 2022[1]). The resilience of the country in face of serious recent economic shocks is testament to the prudent and agile policy response of the authorities, as well as the country's position to benefit from higher international prices for key exports such as gold. Nevertheless, the growth outlook is uncertain, with the continuation of Russia's war in Ukraine and the associated potential for further sanctions to affect Uzbekistan's trade, persistently high domestic inflation and tighter global financial conditions all contributing to a challenging short-to-medium term context.

The resilience of Uzbekistan's economy continues to be hampered by a relatively underdeveloped private sector. Understanding the issues that prevent the private sector from investing, hiring, and growing will be key to improving the resilience of the country in the years ahead. It will also be key to the success of Uzbekistan in navigating the twin transitions of digitalisation and decarbonisation. To this end, the report brings together recent OECD analysis on key business climate issues in the country in order to focus policy attention on the most pressing questions facing the business community in the country.

The content of the report is guided by a survey of international – primarily European – firms operating in Uzbekistan. The survey was an opportunity to gauge business sentiment among a small cohort of international firms of the type that the government is actively seeking to attract to the country. The concerns, observations and positive appraisals gathered through the survey largely dovetail with the OECD's own analysis on business climate issues in Uzbekistan.

1.1.1. The global economic context is undergoing significant transformation

The government must address domestic private sector issues in a global economic context that is undergoing significant transformation, which has implications for the direction, speed and rationale of reforms in Uzbekistan. The global push for more sustainable modes of economic production and organisation is changing the role that governments require the private sector to play in our economies. No longer does the rationale stop at job creation and productivity; firms must also become engines of the decarbonisation transition, investing in the technologies, knowledge and infrastructure needed to address climate challenges. The interconnectedness of global trade, and the gradual introduction of policies such as the EU Carbon Border Adjustment Mechanism, are also indicative of the connection between Uzbekistan's industrial sustainability and its future competitiveness.

The digital transformation of the global economy is changing the how, what, and where of production and business organisation. Digitalisation has major potential benefits for Uzbekistan, for example by creating opportunities for productivity growth and innovation within the public and private sectors, or by improving the efficiency of public services and transparency. Like the sustainability transition, digitalisation has major implications for inclusivity, since being able to benefit from digital technologies – whether at the level of the individual or the firm – depends on access to the knowledge, technology and skills needed to harness them.

1.1.2. Improving the business climate is key to Uzbekistan's ability to tackle the twin transition

The ability of the private sector to harness the opportunities of the twin transition of digitalisation and environmental sustainability is markedly constrained by prevailing weaknesses in the business climate. That improving the business climate has been such a long-standing yet unfulfilled ambition of the Government of Uzbekistan is testament to the difficulty of the task. What constitutes a strong "business climate" is in reality a complex interconnection of numerous different policy areas, with differing responsibilities and rationales for policy intervention. One of the major challenges is therefore ensuring that those responsible for these various policy areas – competition, fiscal, investment, education, environment, labour – are pushing in the same direction. Weaknesses in one, such as competition, can undermine the most successful of efforts in others.

Enabling the private sector to contribute meaningfully to competitiveness, resilience and sustainability requires addressing the numerous barriers to doing business that persist in Uzbekistan. Equally, in the context of the twin transitions of sustainability and digitalisation, the private sector needs additional inputs and support from policymakers. The ongoing reform process to support private sector development and investment, under way since 2017, must therefore go in tandem with policies that support the ability of the private sector to contribute to a range of complex sustainability objectives.

The OECD has worked extensively on policy issues that concern ongoing reforms to support the domestic and international private sector in Uzbekistan, as well as on how global shocks have affected its economy and the broader Central Asian (OECD, 2022[2]) (OECD, 2022[3]) (OECD, 2021[4]) (OECD, 2019[5]). The OECD has also conducted extensive work on how these transitional processes are affecting the countries of Central Asia, for example through recent work on digital skills in Uzbekistan, or hotspot analysis of sustainable infrastructure needs for economic decarbonisation (OECD, 2023[6]) (OECD, 2019[7]).

1.1.3. Findings from the survey dovetail with OECD analysis on business climate issues in Uzbekistan

This report draws upon a private sector survey to shed insights on some of the key business climate issues in Uzbekistan. The survey was a small but focused, addressed to52 firms active in Uzbekistan, the majority of which are entirely or partly owned by entities based in the European Union. The survey presented an opportunity to gather bottom-up, firm-level perceptions on policy issues relating to the business climate and private-sector development in Uzbekistan. The survey The findings of the survey are largely congruent with previous OECD work on business climate issues in Uzbekistan and reinforce the need for reform progress in a number of areas:

- **Additional reforms to support trade facilitation and export promotion would help the development of the country's internationally oriented private-sector**. The "market-seeking" aspect of foreign investors' decisions to enter Uzbekistan underscores the importance of reforms that facilitate trade, both within the country and between Uzbekistan and its neighbours. Similarly, additional support for the country's SMEs could help them identify and access new markets abroad.
- **Firms are positive about the direction of reform to support the business climate, but they require additional pro-competition reforms to benefit from the country's process of liberalisation**. Respondents recognise major progress over the past five years in tackling certain issues that have long beset the local business climate, notably those relating to licensing and registration. At the same time, firms report that there remain significant challenges around key aspects of the business climate, particularly in areas surrounding competition policy and its implementation.

- **Respondents are optimistic about the opportunities that digitalisation presents in Uzbekistan, but private sector digitalisation is held back by insufficient infrastructure investment and skills development.** A large number of respondents report that they have adopted and are using digital technologies but note that opportunities in the digital economy are diminished due to the insufficient development of connectivity infrastructure, low investment in information communication technologies, and underdeveloped digital skills in the labour force.

A fourth thread emerges from the survey that, whilst not directly addressed in this report, gives important additional context to the other areas that are addressed. Responses to the survey suggest that firms in Uzbekistan are aware of the opportunities and challenges of the sustainability transition. A significant plurality report that they are actively adopting new technologies and operations to reduce their carbon footprints and support the government's stated climate change and sustainability ambitions. At the same time, a majority of firms report that policy support for the green transition remains insufficient, with the majority calling for greater investment in sustainable infrastructure, better environmental standards, and stronger financial incentives for the adoption of greener practices within firms.

Taken together, these insights provide important context for the OECD's ongoing work to support the improvement of the business climate in Uzbekistan and help to corroborate and validate the emphasis placed by the OECD on a number of priority areas for reform for the Uzbek authorities. This includes the importance of improving both the hard and soft infrastructure needed for trade within Uzbekistan and between it and its regional neighbours; the importance of tackling inveterately difficult issues around competition and regulatory enforcement; and the importance of investments in the infrastructure and skills necessary to enable firms to not just be objects of the digital and green transitions, but to be active agents in these structural changes and to benefit from them.

1.1.4. Overview of the report

Chapter 2 introduces key aspects of the economic context, highlighting recent trends in policy and performance and discussing their implications for long-term growth. Chapter 3 then proceeds with an introduction to the survey and some high-level observations.

The remaining Chapters of the report are organised around one of the three key issues outlined above, drawing on both the survey findings and complementary OECD analysis on each of these issues. Chapter 4 proceeds with a short discussion on issues relating to trade facilitation and export promotion. Chapter 5 introduces a brief stocktaking of the ongoing regulatory and legal reform process, highlighting persistent issues relating to competition. Chapter 6 looks at the issue of digital infrastructure and skills for private sector competitiveness.

References

OECD (2023), *Digital Skills for Private Sector Competitiveness: Peer Review of Uzbekistan*, OECD Eurasia Policy Insights, OECD Publishing, Paris. [6]

OECD (2022), *An Introduction to Competition Law and Policy in Uzbeksitan*, OECD Publishing, Paris, https://www.oecd.org/daf/competition/an-introduction-to-competition-law-and-policy-in-uzbekistan.pdf. [3]

OECD (2022), *Weathering Economic Storms in Central Asia*, OECD Publishing, https://www.oecd.org/publications/weathering-economic-storms-in-central-asia-83348924-en.htm. [2]

OECD (2021), *Beyond COVID-19: Prospects for Economic Recovery in Central Asia*, OECD Publishing, Paris, https://www.oecd.org/eurasia/Beyond_COVID%2019_Central%20Asia.pdf. [4]

OECD (2019), *Improving the Legal Environment for Business and Investment in Central Asia*, OECD Publishing, Paris, https://www.oecd.org/eurasia/Improving-LEB-CA-ENG%2020%20April.pdf. [5]

OECD (2019), *Uzbekistan*, Sustainable Infrastructure for Low-Carbon Development in Central Asia and the Caucasus, OECD Publishing, Paris, https://www.oecd-ilibrary.org/environment/sustainable-infrastructure-for-low-carbon-development-in-central-asia-and-the-caucasus_d1aa6ae9-en. [7]

World Bank (2022), *Europe and Central Asia Economic Update: Social Protection for Recovery*, World Bank, DC, https://www.worldbank.org/en/region/eca/publication/europe-and-central-asia-economic-update. [1]

2 Transformation and structural change in Uzbekistan's economy

The government of Uzbekistan launched a wide-ranging programme of reforms in 2017 in order to accelerate the transition to an open, market-based economy. The country is now on a pathway to a sounder economic and fiscal footing, but the success of these strategic ambitions depends on the resolution of long-standing issues in the business climate. Addressing these issues is also critical to enabling the broader structural transformation of the country's economy, which despite having started in the mid-1990s, remains at a relatively early stage.

2.1. Private sector development amid stalled structural transformation

The structural transformation of Uzbekistan's economy that began in 1991 remains at a relatively early stage. In large part, this stems from limited success in reorienting resources – human and capital – from historically important sectors characterised by low levels of job creation and productivity to newer, more productive uses. While the value added of agriculture as a percentage of GDP has decreased from 27% in 2010 to 25% in 2021, it remains the highest level in Central Asia, and significantly higher than Kazakhstan (5%) and the OECD average (1%). By contrast, the value added of manufacturing has doubled from 10% to 20% of GDP over the same period, higher than both Kazakhstan (14%) and the OECD average (13%) (Figure 2.1)

Figure 2.1. Value added of the agricultural, manufacturing and service sectors (% GDP)

Uzbekistan has had some progress with structural transformation over the past decade

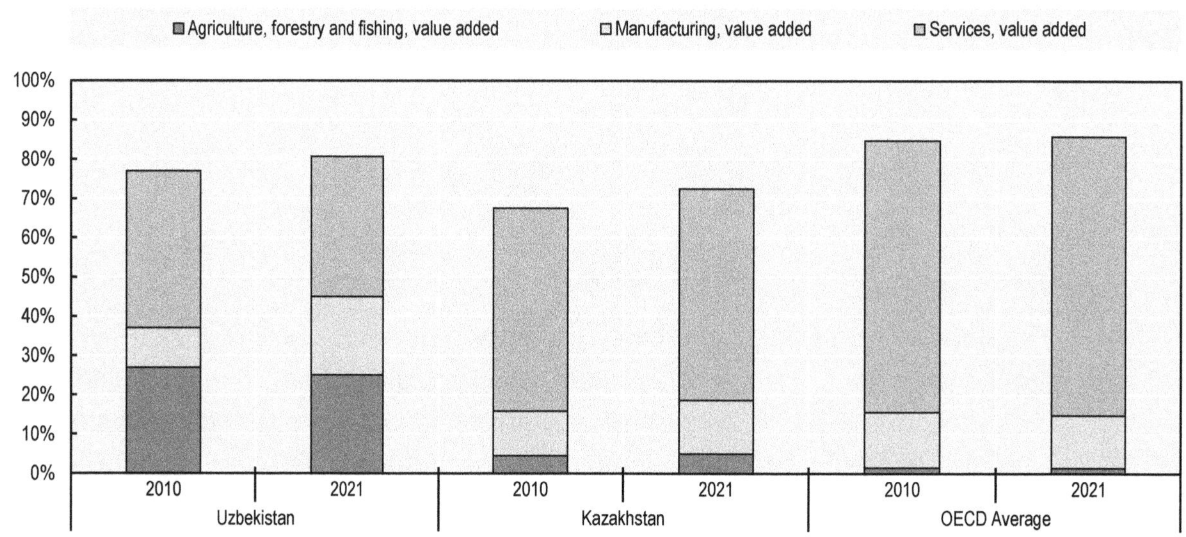

Note: Value added by industries in current USD prices
Source: (UN, 2023[1]) (World Bank, 2023[2])

The weight of services in value creation remains limited. In 2021, the value added of the services sector amounted to 35.7%, the second lowest in Central Asia after Tajikistan (35.3%), and significantly below the OECD average of 71%. This is a lower level than the equivalent figure in 2010 (40%) and indicates a divergence with the other major Central Asian economy, Kazakhstan, where the services share grew from 52% to 54% over the same period. These figures indicate that, while recent efforts to liberalise the economy are significant and positive steps, there remains a great deal of work to do with the structural transformation of the country to one where more people are employed in higher rather than lower productivity sectors.

The distribution of employment similarly attests to challenges with structural change and difficulties in achieving growth that is inclusive. Over 80% of the population are employed in sectors where productivity is half or below half of the national average (Figure 2.2), though the high degree of economic informality in Uzbekistan – particularly in low productivity sectors such as trade and agriculture – that persists in the country may mean that there are in fact more workers in lower productivity activities than official data suggest. The agricultural sector accounts for 27% of total employment, with value added per worker averaging UZS 42.5 million (around USD 3780); the agricultural share in employment is the second highest in the region behind Tajikistan (46%) and significantly higher than the OECD average of 5%. At the same time, the sectors with the highest levels of productivity – real estate activities, financial and insurance services, mining, ICT – account for a very small proportion of employment. The challenge for policymakers is ensuring that the benefits of strong macroeconomic performance of the country are distributed throughout society in a way which is inclusive and underpins social cohesion.

Figure 2.2. Value added per worker and sectoral share of employment, 2020 (in UZS)

High-productivity sectors account for a small share of total employment

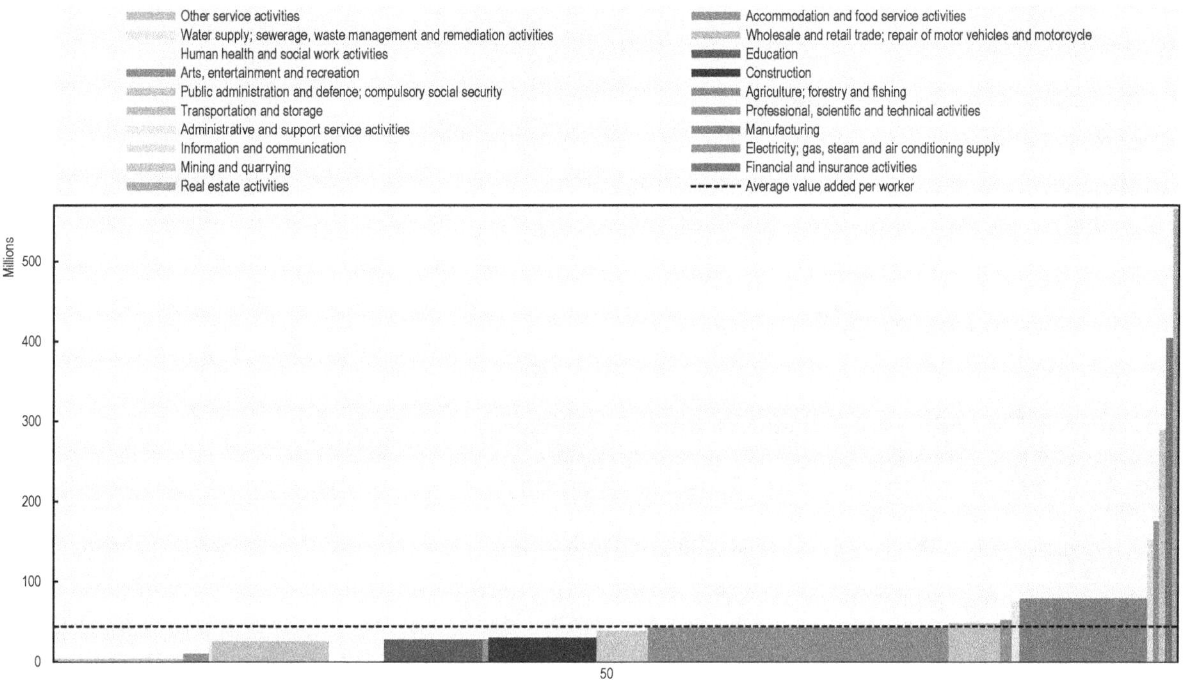

Note: Horizontal axis runs 0-100%. It is important to note that the chart does not show informal employment, which remains significant in Uzbekistan as in other countries in Central Asia.
Source: OECD calculations based (ILO, 2023[3]) and (UN, 2023[1])

As in other Central Asian economies, there is a link between the depth and resilience of structural change and diversification. To a significant extent, the expansion of Uzbekistan's service sector – whether it is job creation in high-value services like finance or lower-value ones like retail and hospitality – has been driven by rents from the trade of minerals and migrant labour. This is not to diminish successes in creating high-quality service sector jobs in Uzbekistan, but to highlight the link between diversification and the resilience of the non-tradable sector.

Since the government began a programme of market liberalisation in 2016/17, business dynamism has significantly increased. Following several years of relatively stagnant enterprise growth, the number of firm entries – the creation of new firms in the economy – grew rapidly from 2016, with a particular acceleration from 2018 onwards (Figure 2.3). At the same time, the number of firm exits – the liquidation or bankruptcy of previously active firms – fell markedly. Trends in firm growth were disrupted by the COVID-19 pandemic, with the number of firms exiting the market growing precipitously in 2020-21, though the number of new firms continued to grow during this period. The industries in which the highest rates of firm creation have been observed are in (retail) trade, industry, and agriculture.

Figure 2.3. Business dynamism in Uzbekistan

The growth of new firms is rising, driven mainly by dynamism in non-tradable sectors of the economy

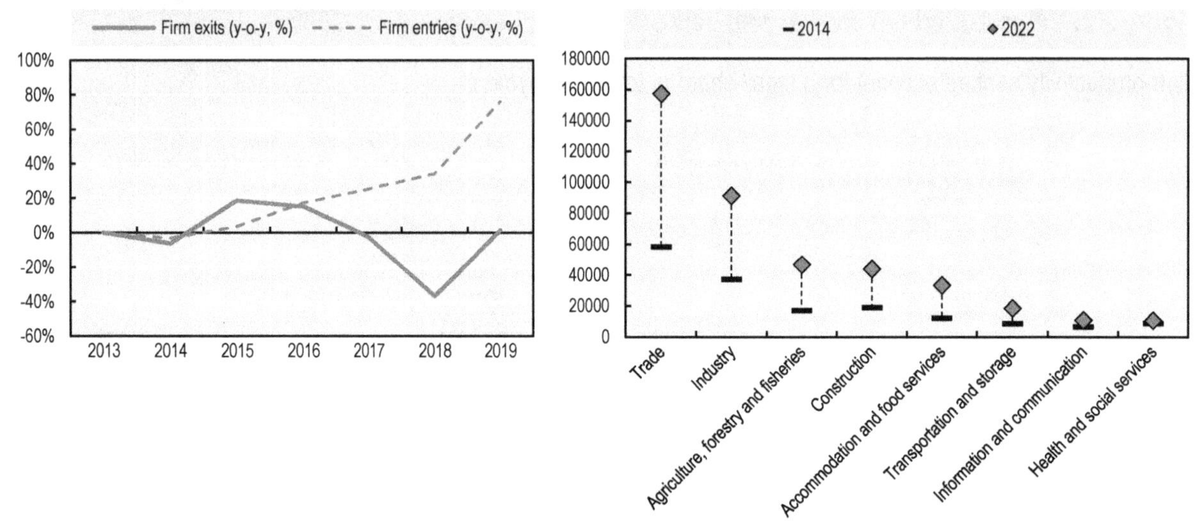

Note: Data from 2020 and 2021 have been omitted from panel 1 due to the exceptional number rate of firm exits (enterprise liquidations) that occurred that year, though in actual terms firm entries (creations) still significantly exceeded exits; 2013 = 0. Panel 2 shows the change in the number of enterprises by economic activity, running left to right on the horizontal access based on the magnitude of change between 2014 and 2022; data for 'other industries' have been omitted.
Source: OECD calculations based on Uzbekistan's enterprise data (The State Committee of the Republic of Uzbekistan on Statistics, 2023[4])

High-growth firms (in particular start-ups) tend to be concentrated in service sectors, and it is precisely in a number of these sectors where the lowest rates of firm creation have been seen in Uzbekistan. Nevertheless, the generally positive trends in business dynamism take place in the context of an extensive programme of market liberalisation, a large part of which has focussed on making it easier to start and close a business. In addition to the regulatory environment, there are a number of factors that can affect business dynamism, many of which are relevant to both the BCA and to other areas of OECD work in the country: integration into global value chains (GVCs), access to finance, occupational standards and labour market regulation all play a role (OECD, 2021[5]).

The weight of small and medium sized enterprises (SMEs) and private entrepreneurship in the economy has increased since 2000. In 2000, 4.5 million workers were employed in SMEs, and SME output accounted for 31% of GDP. By 2021, SME employment had grown to 10.1 million, equal to 86% of total employment, and SME output accounted for 54.9% of GDP. Nevertheless, a burgeoning SME sector does not necessarily equate to private sector development, since many SMEs are in essence state-owned enterprises (SOEs), with the share of truly private firms difficult to ascertain from official statistics.

Figure 2.4. SME share in trade, GDP and employment (2000-2021)

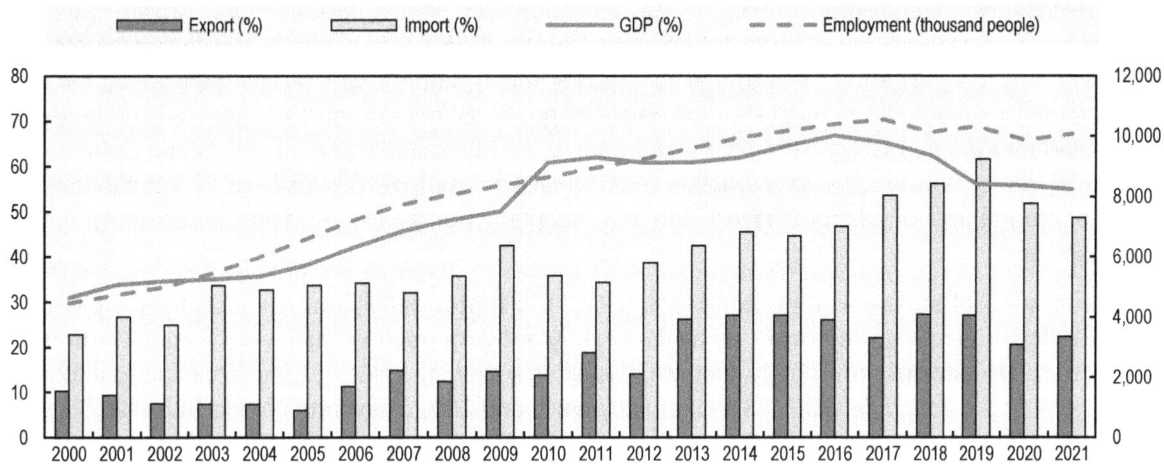

Source: OECD calculations based on data from (The State Committee of the Republic of Uzbekistan on Statistics, 2023[4])

The contribution of SMEs to trade is growing, but firm internationalisation is held back by productivity challenges. From 2000 to 2021, the share of SMEs in imports doubled from 22.8% to 48.7%, while their share of exports grew from 10.2% to 22.3% (Figure 2.4). This historical trade deficit may partly be explained by the sectoral distribution of SMEs in the economy and their productivity level, with many of Uzbekistan's SMEs' being concentrated in low-productivity sectors an impediment to trade (Melitz, 2003[6]). The widening deficit in recent years may also be a factor of firms importing larger amounts of capital goods to upgrade and modernise their capacities. As of 2023, there remains insufficient data on the extent of indirect exports to Russia, i.e., the share of trade with Russia where Uzbekistan acts as an intermediary between a third market and Russia. In 2022, 97.2% of all firms in agriculture were SMEs, while the figure for construction was 74.9%, with these two sectors being characterised by low levels of productivity. In contrast, the most significant sectoral share of newly registered SMEs in the first half of 2022 was trade (36.9%) and industry (18.9%), indicating a trend of positive firm growth in higher productivity, export-orientated sectors.

Uzbekistan is experiencing rapid demographic expansion, raising the importance of quality job creation and labour market inclusion. The economy creates around 280,000 new jobs per year on average, less than half of the 600,000 new jobs required to keep up with labour force expansion (World Bank, 2019[7]). Following the beginning of Russia's war in Ukraine, Uzbekistan has also seen significant inflows of highly skilled Russian migrants (OECD, 2022[8]). In the absence of sufficient job creation, labour migration will likely persist. Remittances from labour migrants, amounting to 13.3% of GDP in 2021, remain an important driver of household consumption (particularly for food products), but their importance for consumption also raises the economic exposure of Uzbekistan to downswings in key external labour markets, such as Russia (OECD, 2022[8]). At the same time, levels of urbanisation in Uzbekistan remain low – this is something that the government acknowledges. A Presidential Decree from 2019 called for the rate of urbanisation to increase to 60% by 2030 (ILO, 2021[9]). People and capital generally gravitate to places of greater economic potential, but barriers to the reallocation of land (for example, to construct more affordable housing in urban centres, a major barrier for many looking to move to major cities), capital, and labour can all distort this process. The ongoing government consultation to remove the *propiska* system (a system of internal permissions for labour mobility, which has historically been an impediment to rural-urban internal migration) could significantly alleviate constraints on urban migration (Seitz, 2020[10]).

There is significant progress yet to be made on the process of the transformation of the state as from the primary producer of economic output to an enabler of it. The government is gradually beginning to refashion its role in economic development as an enabler of private sector development and investment, for example, by improving the framework conditions – skills, access to finance, infrastructure, etc. – necessary for entrepreneurship. Historically, however, industrialisation and growth have been overwhelmingly state-directed. The consequences of this model for current challenges facing private sector development are significant. For one, due to a policy focus before 2017 on self-sufficiency, economic development was promoted through state-owned enterprises (SOEs), which were generally protected from competition through regulatory exemptions and often were monopolies in their respective sectors. In the agricultural sector, the focus was extractive and did little to improve productivity. The authorities have begun a programme of corporatisation and privatisation, though this remains at an early stage of implementation.

The dominance of state-owned enterprises (SOEs) in historically important sectors – principally mineral extraction and agriculture – as well as in key network sectors, has been a major impediment to structural transformation. The output of Uzbekistan's roughly 2,000 (SOEs) continue to account for around 50% of the country's GDP, 18% of employment, and 20% of exports (World Bank, 2022[11]). The footprint of SOEs also varies significantly across regions, with the contribution of SOEs to regional output ranging from 26% in the Namangan region to 80% in Navoi and Karakalpakstan (Abdullaev, 2020[12]). Estimates for the true scale of the presence of the state vary, often upwards, owing in large part to difficulties with statistical collection and classifications (the authorities and statistical agencies only consider 'state unitary enterprises' with 100% state ownership to be SOEs, masking a vast number of companies with partial – often majority – state ownership, and thereby understating the true footprint of the state in the economy). A 2014 World Bank report, for example, calculated that 37% of the workforce were employed in SOEs, with another 34% self-employed, meaning that SOE employment accounted for over half of total wage employment in the country (World Bank, 2014[13]). The presence of SOEs in the banking sector is considerable, with state-owned banks holding 88% of all outstanding credit in the country at the end of 2020 (World Bank, 2022[11]). Despite the lack of clarity, there is a general consensus that the presence is large enough to force nascent market institutions to the margins of the economy, where their ability to shape the socio-economic direction of Uzbekistan will be limited (Abdullaev, 2020[12]).

The interaction between the pervasive presence of SOEs in the economy and structural transformation is complex and multifaceted. In a context where the government is actively seeking to foster the creation of high-quality jobs for a rapidly expanding labour force, the extensive presence of SOEs creates a myriad of challenges that will continue to frustrate private sector development: soft budgetary constraints on SOEs contribute to inefficiencies, poor governance of incumbents, subsidies to support below cost-recovery services and the impact on investment. Taken together, the extent of SOE presence in the economy, the poor governance and oversight of many of these enterprises, and the location of these SOEs in key network sectors, all contribute to make the playing field for business uneven, limiting the effectiveness of otherwise encouraging reform efforts to improve the business and investment climate in the country.

2.2. Growth, trade and investment: relevant economic trends for private sector development

From a macroeconomic perspective, Uzbekistan has made significant progress since beginning its transition to a market economy in the early 1990s. Since Uzbekistan emerged from the post-transition recession in 1996, Uzbekistan's real GDP has grown by an average annual rate of 5.9%, above the regional average of 5.3% (World Bank, 2023[2]). Gross FDI stocks in the last pre-pandemic year of 2019 equaled 16.6% GDP, an four-fold increase since 2000, while net inflows were equal to 3.9% GDP, an increase of 680% and 35% over the same period as above (UNCTAD, 2023[14]) (World Bank, 2023[2]). From 2010 to 2021, there was a sevenfold increase in labour productivity, measured in terms of value added per worker in million UZS, while levels of poverty, the reduction of which is a key ambition of the government, have fallen by 88% since 2000 (measured as the percentage of employed living on below USD 1.9 PPP per day). In 2021, unemployment fell from 10.5% to 9.4%, a level that Uzbekistan had generally sustained in the years preceding the pandemic. External debt reached 57.8% GDP in 2021, below the legal threshold of 60%, with this having expanded significantly in recent years (IMF, 2022[15]).

Gross fixed capital formation (GFCF) has made a major contribution to growth in recent years (Fig. 2.4b). GFCF has primarily been driven by public investment, with levels of domestic private and foreign direct investment remaining low (IMF, 2022[15]). For the domestic private sector, access to finance remains a key challenge, in part due to the underdevelopment of the national banking sector and pervasive role of the state therein; for larger firms, the underdevelopment of local capital markets is an additional barrier. SMEs suffer from particularly difficult access to finance conditions, owing in large part to demanding collateralisation requirements and the high cost of credit, with some 64% of SMEs reliant on internal resources for investment (OECD, 2021[16]). Credit to the private sector as a percentage of GDP has grown significantly since 2016, going from the lowest in Central Asia (11.8%) to the highest (35.7%), though this remains far below the OECD average of 160.7% GDP and has been accompanied by a rapid increase in non-performing loans (NPLs). An additional constraint is the difficulty in differentiating between lending growth to the real private sector and growth to enterprises with differing degrees of state control (World Bank, 2023[17]).

The collapse of investment – public and private – following the COVID-19 pandemic had an immediate and significant impact on real GDP growth, though trend growth remains positive (Figure 2.5 a). Since 2019, the contribution of GFCF to GDP growth remains subdued, and tighter global monetary conditions will make it more difficult for the state to remain the country's lead investor, raising the importance of policy support for domestic lending and FDI attraction. At the same time, the role of household consumption as a contributor to growth has expanded significantly (Figure 2.5 b).

Figure 2.5. Real GDP growth and contributions to growth

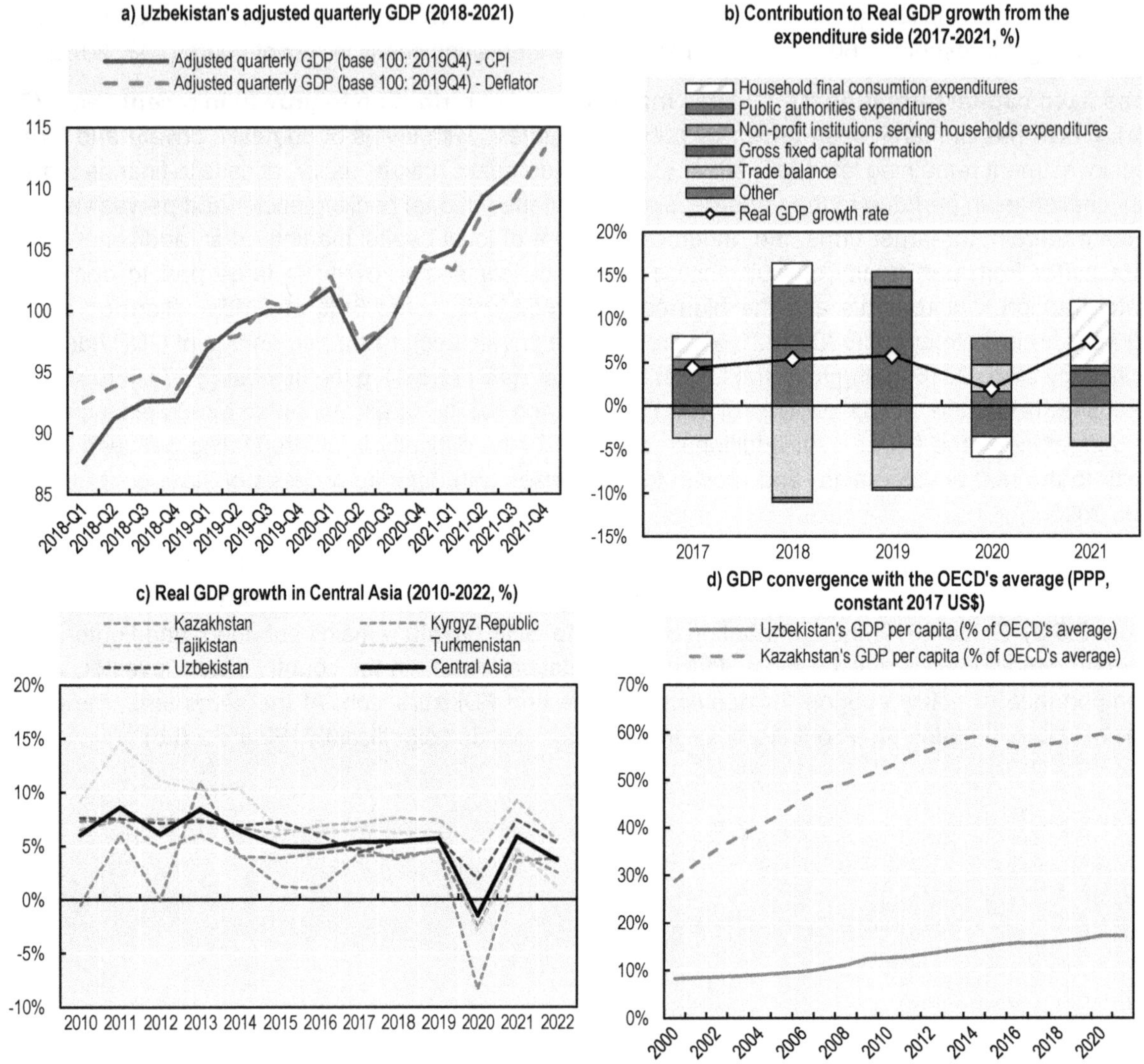

Source: Panels A and B, OECD calculations based on national accounts data from State Committee of the Republic of Uzbekistan on Statistics (The State Committee of the Republic of Uzbekistan on Statistics, 2023[18]); Panels C and D OECD calculations based on World Bank data (World Bank, 2023[2])

Whilst it is important not to diminish Uzbekistan's economic performance, the country's generally strong post-transition macroeconomic trends follow an established convergence trajectory. The economic development literature suggests that capital-scarce emerging economies grow faster than capital-rich developed countries because of diminishing marginal returns to investment, to which an early part of Uzbekistan's economic performance may be attributable (Abramovitz, 1986[19]) (Barro and Sala-i-Martin, 2004[20]). Against this longer-term trend, the COVID-19 pandemic and Russia's war in Ukraine actually came on the back of a challenging decade. Buffeted by a series of powerful external shocks – the Global Financial Crisis in 2008-09 and then the end of the commodity price boom in 2014-15, which affected the country through its deep trade and labour linkages with Russia – it appeared that the commodity-driven and cyclical growth paths that were prevalent throughout the region had begun to run out of steam: growth remained strong but was slowing (Figure 2.5 c), and convergence with OECD countries has begun to stagnate; the convergence gap with Kazakhstan has also continued to widen (Figure 2.5 d) (OECD, 2021[21]).

The reform process that started in Uzbekistan in 2017 was in part in response to the need to do things differently to achieve sustainable, inclusive, and resilient growth. The basic premise of these reforms was to enable the private sector to play a larger role in the economy, to diminish the role of the state in the economy, and to improve the country's economic buffers. Early macroeconomic indicators suggest that these reforms may already have started to put the country's economy on a sounder economic and fiscal footing. Between 2017 and 2019, Uzbekistan recorded average annual growth of 5.2%, slightly below the Central Asia average of 5.5%. Stronger fundamentals, good policy buffers – a low public debt to GDP ratio (though one that has risen significantly in recent years), strong international reserves, remittances, etc. – together with high gold prices (a key export) have enabled the country to mitigate the worst of the pandemic (IMF, 2022[15]) (OECD, 2021[21]). In 2022, the economy again appears to have performed relatively well in absorbing the shock of Russia's war in Ukraine, with GDP growth in 2022 of 5.2%, though this in part may be due to certain one-off factors such as the rapid increase in household consumption.

Although Uzbekistan has one of the most energy-intensive economies in the world, the country is increasing the productivity of emissions and energy consumption relative to growth. Uzbekistan's CO2 intensity – the volume of CO2 required to produce 1 USD PPP of output – fell almost 75% between 2000 and 2020, but current levels (0.43kg CO2/USD PPP) remain 77% above the world average (Figure 2.6 a) (IEA, 2022[22]). At the same time, 1 tonne equivalent of oil (TOE) in Uzbekistan produced USD 5,524 of output in 2020, a level, whilst much higher than in 2000 (e.g., the same 1 TOE would have produced less output in 2000), remains far below the OECD average, where the equivalent TOE would produce twice as much output (Figure 2.6 b). The persistently high levels of CO2 emissions and energy required for Uzbekistan's growth is due to a number of energy-intensive industries and the dominance of fossil fuels in the country's energy supply (Figure 2.6 d). Nevertheless, the cost of inefficiency and emissions are profound for both the government and society of Uzbekistan. The OECD Environment Directorate estimates that Uzbekistan has by far the highest level of premature deaths due to particulate matter (PM2.5) exposure in Central Asian (around 800 per 1,000,000 inhabitants), and that the welfare costs of premature mortality due to exposure to PM2.5 pollution amount to around 10% GDP in 2019 (OECD, 2022[23]).

Figure 2.6. CO2 and energy intensity of Uzbekistan's economy

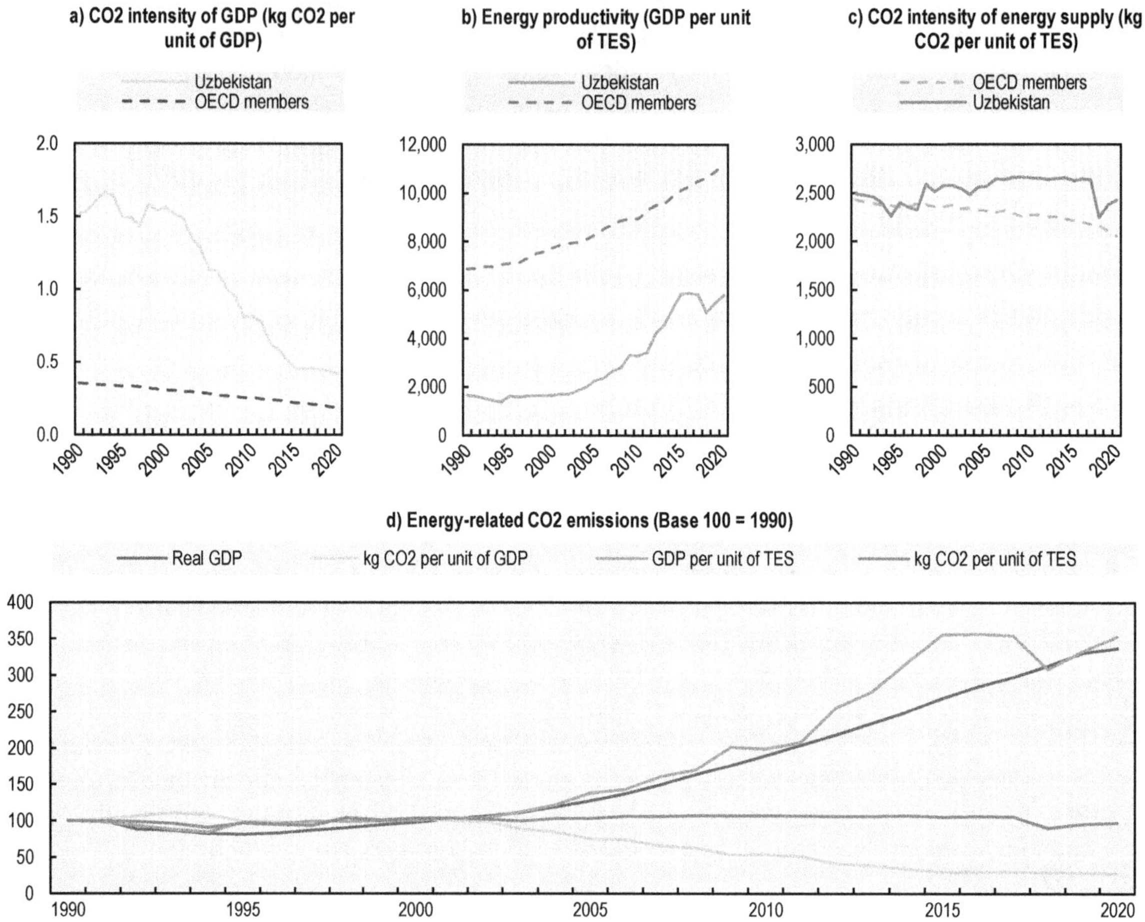

Note: Units: GDP is expressed in USD, 2015.
Source: (OECD, 2023[24])

Reforms to support international trade were a major component of the broader reform process that began in 2017, with the recent resumption of accession talks between Uzbekistan and the WTO a further indication of the country's internationalisation. Since 2016, trade as a percentage of GDP has more than doubled from 29% of GDP – at that point the lowest level in Central Asia – to 64% in 2019, though part of this increase may be attributable to currency liberalisation reforms. The country continues to run a sizable trade deficit, one which in recent years may have widened due to the need to invest in capital goods to modernise and expand the industrial base. Exports are dominated by low-tech, largely primary goods: gold, cotton, and some additional mineral and fuel products account for the largest share of the country's export basket (Figure 2.7). In contrast, medium- and high-tech products account for a very small share of exports, indicating either a low-level of export-orientation of these industries or a lack of the more knowledge- and technology-intensive capacities necessary to develop them.

Figure 2.7. Structure of trade: export basket and partners

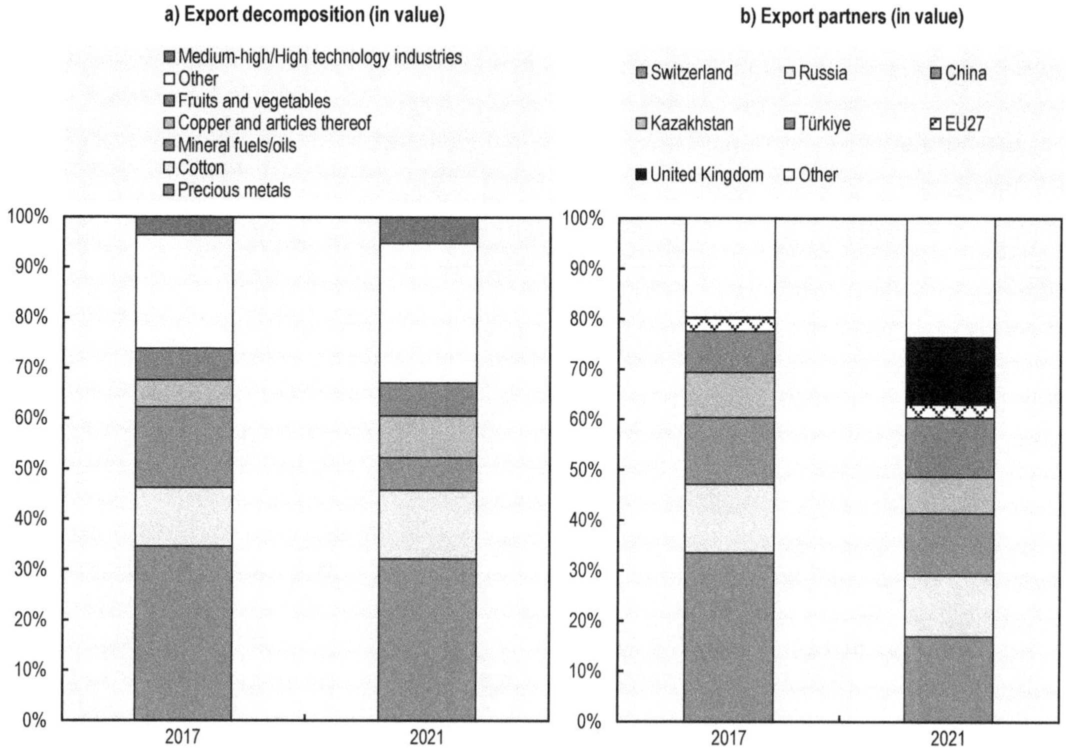

Note: Medium-high/High technologies classification have been computed according to the ISIC REV.3 Technology Intensity Definition (OECD, 2011). Among the "Other" category, the top three exported products are textile, plastics and articles thereof and finally fertilizers.
Source: OECD calculations based on data from (UN Comtrade, 2023[25])

In 2021, Switzerland was Uzbekistan's largest export market, accounting for 17% of the country's exports. The significant share of Switzerland as a share of Uzbekistan's export partners reflects the importance of the European country for the refining of gold, as well as the importance of gold in Uzbekistan's exports, with 99.9% of Uzbekistan's exports to the Swiss market accounted for by the precious metal. Other major export partners include the United Kingdom (13.3% of exports), China (12.4%), and Russia (12.1%). The composition of the country's export basket varies significantly depending on the country, with exports to the United Kingdom, as with Switzerland, being almost entirely gold. In contrast, exports to other markets, such as China, Russia and Turkey, are more varied, though primary and low-technology content goods predominate. Given the connectivity penalty Uzbekistan suffers, it is unsurprising that its largest trading partners for lower value-to-weight goods are geographically proximate. The share of exports to the EU27 remains small (2.7%), though this figure may rise in the years ahead following the introduction of a Generalised Scheme of Preferences (GSP+) trade facilitation agreement between the EU and Uzbekistan in April 2021.

Owing in large part to a highly restrictive investment regulation, FDI levels in Uzbekistan have historically been much lower than other countries in Central Asia. Yet, since around 2014, FDI as a share of GDP and as a share of total GFCF have been trending upwards, whilst the reverse has been true of the broader region (Figure 2.8) This in part reflects the easing of strict investment and currency regulations that had deterred foreign investors from entering Uzbekistan, though it perhaps also is reflective of the types of opportunities available to investors in Uzbekistan relative to other regional economies, such as the size of the domestic market. Increasing the share of FDI in Uzbekistan's GFCF is a key aim of the government, but success will depend both on addressing long-standing issues facing the domestic business climate as well as other regulatory and structural issues that are particularly challenging for international investors, such as the lack of a developed domestic capital market and a lack of co-financing vehicles such as public-private partnerships (PPPs).

Figure 2.8. Foreign direct investment in Uzbekistan

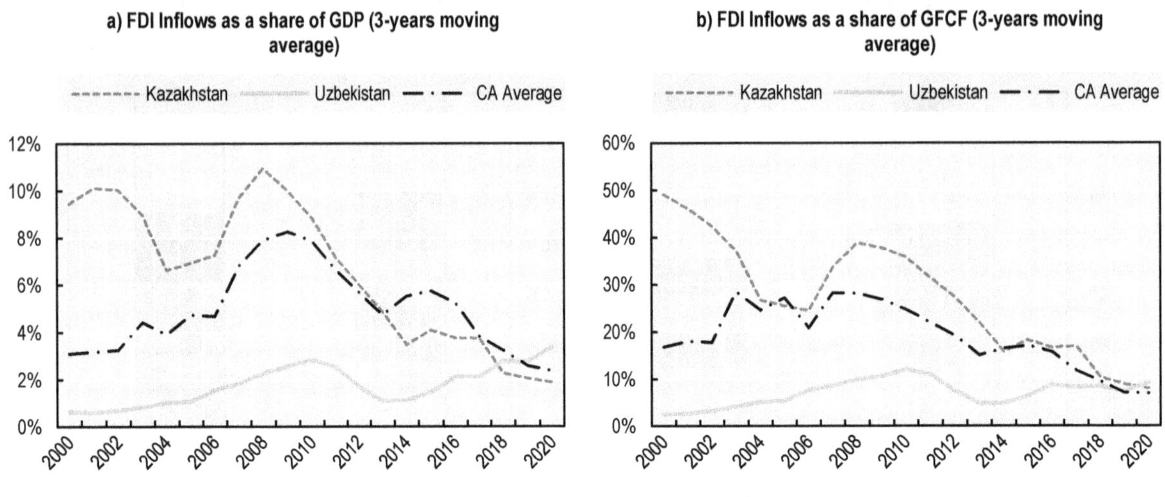

Source: OECD calculations based on data from (UNCTAD, 2023[26])

While Uzbekistan has so far managed the economic spillovers of Russia's war in Ukraine relatively well, a prolonged conflict could pose serious challenges to socio-economic wellbeing in Uzbekistan remain substantial. Russia continues to account for over 20% of imports and 12% exports, while much of Uzbekistan's external trade passes through Russia – underdeveloped trade connectivity between Uzbekistan and other regions means that external trade risks becoming more complicated and more expensive for the country (IMF, 2022[15]). Another important channel that affects Uzbekistan is remittances, levels of which remained close to 10% GDP in 2021 and of which almost 75% originated in Russia. One in six households in Uzbekistan relies upon remittances as the primary income source and account on average for 20% of household incomes (Ibid.). As in other areas of the world, rising commodity prices – notably food (wheat) and fuel) – may feed into inflation, which remained over 10% throughout 2022 (OECD, 2022[27]).

References

Abdullaev, U. (2020), *State-Owned Enterprises in Uzbekistan: Taking Stock and Some Reform Priorities*, ADBI Working Paper Series, No. No. 1068, Asian Development Bank Institute, https://www.adb.org/sites/default/files/publication/560601/adbi-wp1068.pdf. [12]

Abramovitz, M. (1986), *Catching Up, Forging Ahead, and Falling Behind*, The Journal of Economic History, No. Vol. 46, No. 2, Cambridge University Press, https://www.jstor.org/stable/2122171?seq=1. [19]

Barro, R. and X. Sala-i-Martin (2004), *Economic Growth (2nd ed.)*, The MIT Press, http://piketty.pse.ens.fr/files/BarroSalaIMartin2004Chap1-2.pdf. [20]

IEA (2022), *Uzbekistan 2022: Energy Policy Review*, International Energy Agency, Paris, https://iea.blob.core.windows.net/assets/0d00581c-dc3c-466f-b0c8-97d25112a6e0/Uzbekistan2022.pdf. [22]

ILO (2023), *ILOSTAT*, ILO, Geneva, https://ilostat.ilo.org/. [3]

ILO (2021), *Towards Full and Productive Employment in Uzbekistan: Achievements and Challenges*, Employment Country Reports Series, ILO, https://www.ilo.org/wcmsp5/groups/public/---europe/---ro-geneva/---sro-moscow/documents/publication/wcms_782059.pdf. [9]

IMF (2022), *Republic of Uzbekistan: 2022 Article IV Consultation-Press Release; Staff Report; and Statement by the Executive Director for the Republic of Uzbekistan*, IMF, DC, https://www.imf.org/en/Publications/CR/Issues/2022/06/22/Republic-of-Uzbekistan-2022-Article-IV-Consultation-Press-Release-Staff-Report-and-519919. [15]

Melitz, M. (2003), *The Impact of Trade on Intra-Industry Reallocations and Aggregate Industry Productivity*, Econometrica, No. Vol. 71, No. 6 (Nov. 2003), The Econometric Society, https://www.jstor.org/stable/1555536. [6]

OECD (2023), *Green Growth Indicators*, OECD Publishing, Paris, https://stats.oecd.org/Index.aspx?DataSetCode=GREEN_GROWTH. [24]

OECD (2022), *Green Economy Transition in Eastern Europe, the Caucasus and Central Asia: Progress and Ways Forward*, OECD Green Growth Studies, OECD Publishing, Paris, https://www.oecd-ilibrary.org/docserver/c410b82a-en.pdf?expires=1677162424&id=id&accname=ocid84004878&checksum=F2BCEEF95E86BA77A3ACBB7C97571F14. [23]

OECD (2022), *Weathering Economic Storms in Central Asia*, OECD Publishing, https://www.oecd.org/publications/weathering-economic-storms-in-central-asia-83348924-en.htm. [27]

OECD (2022), *Weathering Economic Storms in Central Asia: Initial Impacts of the War in Ukraine*, OECD, Paris, https://www.oecd-ilibrary.org/docserver/83348924-en.pdf?expires=1674661005&id=id&accname=ocid84004878&checksum=D702728E79EA5A3E54D1B3CA7ED454E9. [8]

OECD (2021), *Beyond COVID-19: Prospects for Economic Recovery in Central Asia*, OECD Publishing, Paris, https://www.oecd.org/eurasia/Beyond_COVID%2019_Central%20Asia.pdf. [21]

OECD (2021), *Boosting the Internationalisation of Firms through better Export Promotion Policies in Uzbekistan*, OECD Eurasia Policy Insights, OECD Publishing, Paris, https://www.oecd.org/eurasia/Monitoring_Review_Uzbekistan_ENG.pdf. [16]

OECD (2021), *Understanding Firm Growth: Helping SMEs Scale Up*, OECD Studies on SMEs and Entrepreneurship, OECD Publishing, Paris, https://doi.org/10.1787/fc60b04c-en. [5]

Seitz, W. (2020), *Free Movement and Affordable Housing: Public Preferences for Reform in Uzbekistan*, World Bank Policy Research Working Papers, No. No. 9107, World Bank, DC, https://documents1.worldbank.org/curated/en/595891578495293475/pdf/Free-Movement-and-Affordable-Housing-Public-Preferences-for-Reform-in-Uzbekistan.pdf. [10]

The State Committee of the Republic of Uzbekistan on Statistics (2023), *National Accounts*, The State Committee of the Republic of Uzbekistan on Statistics, Tashkent, https://stat.uz/en/official-statistics/national-accounts. [18]

The State Committee of the Republic of Uzbekistan on Statistics (2023), *Small Business and Entrepreneurship*, The State Committee of the Republic of Uzbekistan on Statistics, Tashkent, https://stat.uz/en/official-statistics/small-business-and-entrepreneurship. [4]

UN (2023), *Value added by industries at current prices (ISIC REV. 4)*, United Nations, New York, http://data.un.org/Data.aspx?d=SNA&f=group_code%3A204. [1]

UN Comtrade (2023), *UN Comtrade Database*, UN Comtrade, Geneva, https://comtrade.un.org/. [25]

UNCTAD (2023), *Foreign direct investment: Inward and outward flows and stock, annual*, UNCTAD, Geneva, https://unctadstat.unctad.org/wds/TableViewer/tableView.aspx?ReportId=96740. [26]

UNCTAD (2023), *UNCTATStat*, UNCTAD, Geneva, https://unctadstat.unctad.org/EN/. [14]

World Bank (2023), *Domestic credit to private sector (% GDP)*, World Bank, DC, https://data.worldbank.org/indicator/FS.AST.CGOV.GD.ZS?end=2020&locations=UZ-KG-TJ-KZ-OE&start=2011&view=chart. [17]

World Bank (2023), *World Bank Development Indicators*, World Bank, DC, https://databank.worldbank.org/source/world-development-indicators. [2]

World Bank (2022), *Uzbekistan: The Second Systematic Country Diagnostic*, World Bank, DC, https://documents1.worldbank.org/curated/en/933471650320792872/pdf/Toward-a-Prosperous-and-Inclusive-Future-The-Second-Systematic-Country-Diagnostic-for-Uzbekistan.pdf. [11]

World Bank (2019), *Toward a New Economy: Uzbekistan Country Economic Update Summer 2019*, World Bank, https://documents1.worldbank.org/curated/en/866501562572675697/pdf/Uzbekistan-Toward-a-New-Economy-Country-Economic-Update.pdf. [7]

World Bank (2014), *The Skills Road: Skills for Employability in Uzbekistan*, World Bank, DC, https://documents1.worldbank.org/curated/en/744581468230693258/pdf/910100WP0P14350d000Uzbekistan0Final.pdf. [13]

3 Survey methodology and findings overview

The purpose of the OECD private sector survey of Uzbekistan, conducted by the OECD in 2022, was to collect new firm-level insights into the ongoing reform process to support the business climate in the country. The survey provides additional input for the OECD and the Government to consider when reflecting on the effectiveness and direction of the reform process. This chapter introduces the survey, its methodology, and a number of high-level observations that emerged from the process.

3.1. Introduction

This chapter introduces the business climate assessment survey for Uzbekistan and outlines some general observations that emerged from the survey. Section 3.2 outlines the methodology of the survey and details how it was administered, with further details available in Annex A to this report, while section 3.3 details the business demography of the sample firms. Section 3.4 then provides additional information on firm perceptions of the current economic trends in Uzbekistan, the impact of COVID-19 and Russia's war of aggression in Ukraine on the business climate in Uzbekistan, and the perceived strengths and limitations of policy interventions to support them during these periods of disruption.

3.2. Survey methodology and administration

The survey was a small but focused survey of 52 firms active in Uzbekistan, with the majority being wholly or partly owned by entities based in the EU. The survey presented an opportunity to gather bottom-up, firm-level perceptions on issues relating to the business climate and private-sector development in Uzbekistan.

The survey was developed by the OECD and administered via an online survey of foreign businesses and their representatives in Chambers of Commerce (CCs) and Embassies. The consultation of primarily European businesses was designed to identify issues of particular importance to international firms in Uzbekistan, the attraction of which remains a priority for the government. Throughout this report, analysis of survey responses, unless otherwise indicated, is based on the responses of both the 52 individual firms and the two organisational respondents.

Characteristics of surveyed firms

The 52 firms that took part in the survey were highly varied in terms of their characteristics (Figure 3.1) Micro, small and medium-sized enterprises (SMEs) were dominant (73%), with this category distributed relatively evenly between micro- (27%), small- (25%), and medium-sized enterprises (21%). Large companies, i.e., those with over 250 employees, accounted for the remaining 27% of survey respondents.

Most firms were relatively new to Uzbekistan. Some 52% of respondents had only been active in Uzbekistan for 0-5 years, perhaps indicative of an improved perception of the country's business climate within the European business community following the reform process begun in 2017. The length of time that firms had been active in Uzbekistan for the other respondents was relatively evenly distributed across 6-10 years (8%), 11-15 years (12%), 16-20 years (12%) and over 21 years (17%).

The ownership and legal structure of the respondents was also varied. The ownership of a large plurality of the surveyed firms (42%) was 100% based in the EU, while another 12% had majority EU ownership. The ownership of the remaining firms was either 100% Uzbek (17%), or from a different jurisdiction or combinations thereof (27%). France accounted for the single largest share of respondents (14, or 25%), followed by Italy (7/12%) and the United Kingdom (6/12%). A large plurality of firms had LLC status (46%), with the remaining firms having a range of different legal statuses, including JSCs (13%) or representative offices (16%).

The respondents represented a diverse range of sectors, and were relatively evenly spread among them. Engineering and construction marginally accounted for the largest single share (8%) of firms, followed by manufacturing (6%), mining, oil and gas extraction (6%), electricity and energy production (6%), machinery (5%) and agriculture (5%). A significant proportion of respondents (36%) belonged to 'other' sectors.

Figure 3.1. Demographics of respondent firms

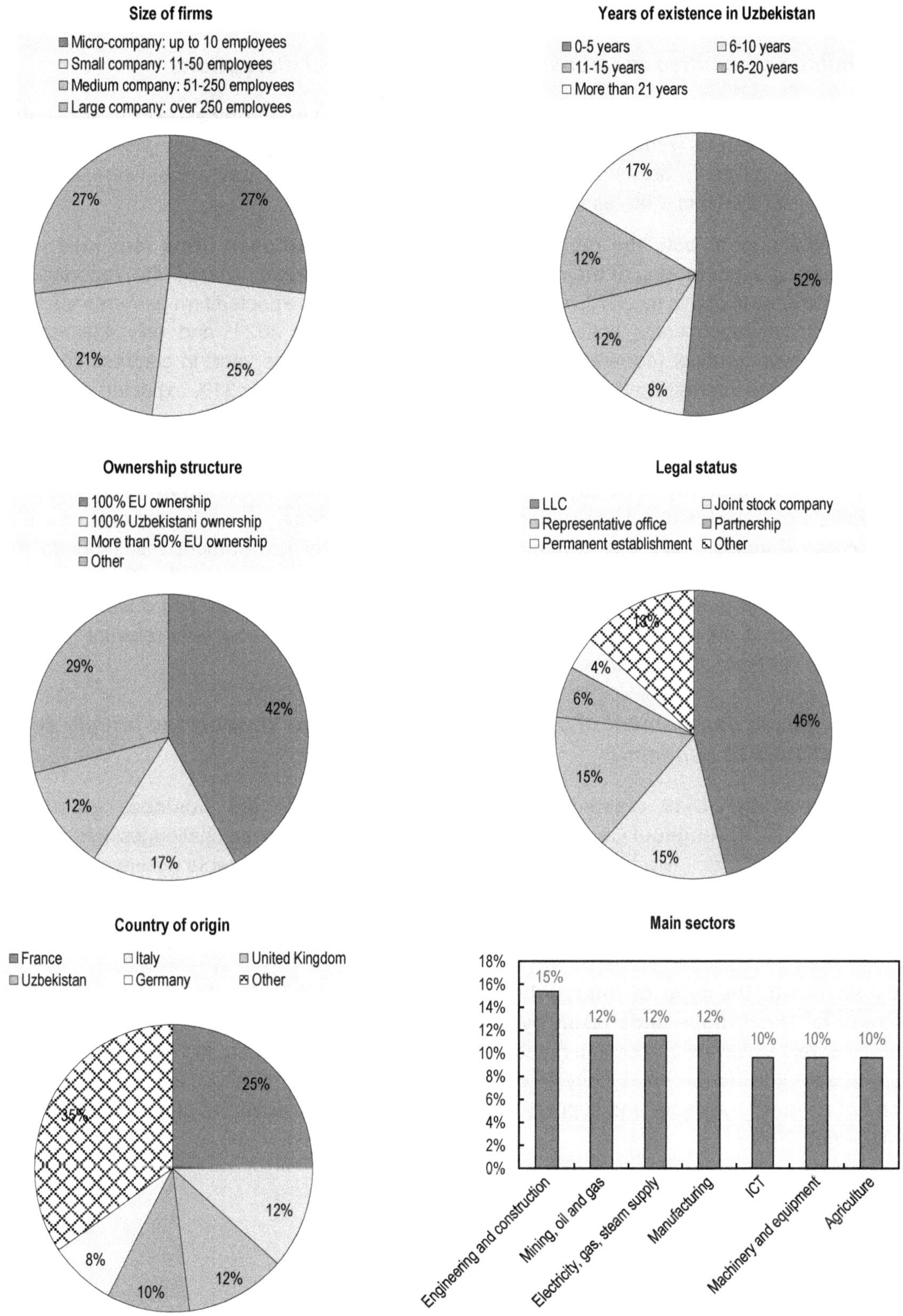

Note: As a percent of the total number of firms.
Source: EU-OECD Business Climate Assessment Survey in Uzbekistan (2022)

3.3. High level observations on economic performance in Uzbekistan and recent policy support

Firms remained committed to Uzbekistan despite external disruptions

A majority of respondents (70%) rated the health of the national economy as satisfactory, with 15% of respondents rating it as weak or and the same number as strong. There was greater positivity from respondents when asked to assess the performance of the sector in which they were active or the performance of their own firm (25% and 29% respectively).

Despite uncertainties at both the regional and global level, European firms remained relatively positive regarding expectations of their own performance. A significant share (44%) reported that they expected an increase in profits for 2022, with 37% reporting that they expected firm performance to remain stable. Only 8% of respondents anticipated decreased profits for 2022, and only 4% reported an expectation for trade turnover (domestic and international) to fall for the year. In contrast, some 25% of respondents expected international trade turnover to increase, and a further 31% expected domestic trade turnover to increase – perhaps reflecting an increase in domestic demand due to a rapid expansion of credit.

This section of the report presents key insights from four sections of the survey. The section covers firm perceptions of government support during the COVID-19 pandemic, of the impact of Russia's war on Ukraine on the European business community in Uzbekistan, of government measures to mitigate pressures on the business community arising due to war-related disruptions, and of the ongoing reform process in Uzbekistan to support the business climate more broadly. The section does not extensively cover every aspect of the survey, instead focusing on those that are particularly relevant for firms and policymakers. A full breakdown of responses can be found in Annex B.

Firms had a mixed assessment of government measures to support the private sector during the COVID-19 pandemic

The outbreak of COVID-19 created significant challenges for the business community in Uzbekistan, as it did throughout Central Asia and the OECD area. These challenges also created new expectations of government, which was called on to ensure the survival of viable businesses and prevent their unnecessary exit from the market. The design and implementation of policy interventions to this end required a high degree of agility from policymakers, who were required to make quick, effective decisions in a context of heightened temporal and fiscal constraints.

Broadly speaking, the type of interventions from Uzbek authorities to support the business community mirrored those undertaken by OECD members, even if they differed in scale. These interventions were widely discussed in a number of OECD reports throughout the height of the pandemic, and the survey provided an opportunity to gauge how European firms assessed the effectiveness of government policies to stabilise and support the private sector throughout the global pandemic (OECD, 2021[1]) (OECD, 2021[2]).

Figure 3.2. Government's measures effectiveness against the COVID-19 pandemic according to the respondents

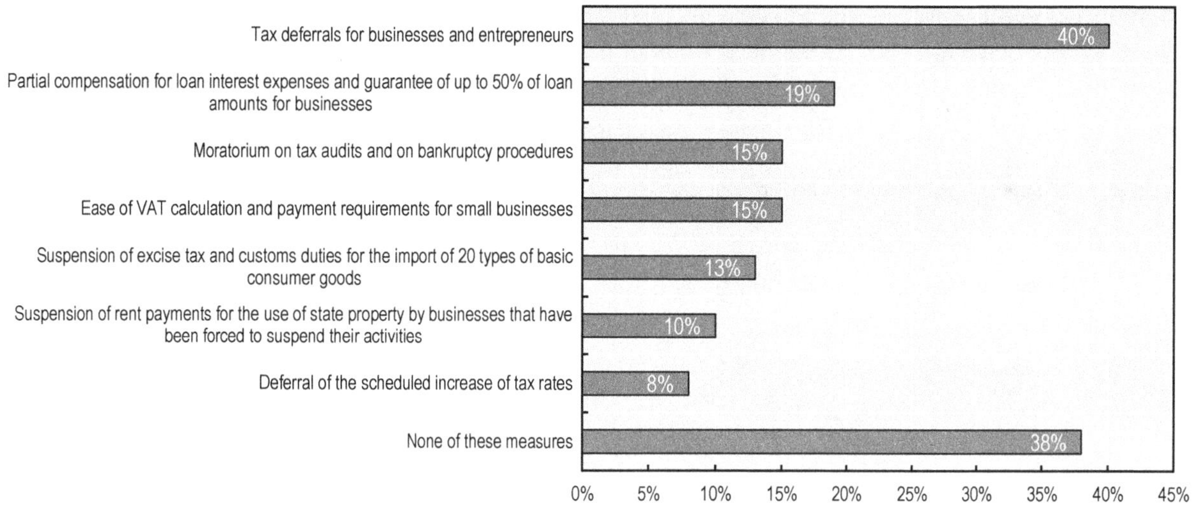

Note: As a percent of the total number of respondents.
Source: EU-OECD Business Climate Assessment Survey on Uzbekistan (2022)

While a significant share of respondents (40%) noted the effectiveness of tax deferrals for businesses and entrepreneurs, it is notable that a similar figure (38%) considered none of the measures listed in the survey to be effective (Figure 3.2).Respondents were not asked to expand upon the reasons for their answers, but that such a relatively high number perceived government measures to be ineffective during the pandemic raises questions regarding the quality of policy design and implementation. At the same time, this was an exceptional period, for the private and public sectors alike, and the heterogeneity of challenges faced by both means it is unlikely that all firms' needs would have been satisfied. In a period of heightened global uncertainty and disruption, the importance for the Uzbek authorities is to identify what enabled policymakers to make effective interventions in a fast-moving environment, and to ensure that lessons from those periods are taken forward.

Firms report agility in dealing with the disruptions caused by Russia's war in Ukraine

Russia's war of aggression in Ukraine delivered another significant shock to the business community in Uzbekistan, both its domestic and international firms. The shocks endured by the local business community were felt via the same channels as in many OECD countries: supply chain disruptions, rising prices for primary and intermediate goods, inflation, and a tightening in the global financial system that has affected international and local borrowing costs. At the same time, these impact channels were mapped over local circumstances that were peculiar to the region: the particularly large importance of Russia as a trading partner and as a route for exports for Central Asian economies, the interconnectedness of Central Asian banking systems with Russia's, the immediate impact of both low- and high-skilled migrants from Russia, the potential for a stagnant Russian economy to affect remittance levels, and the impact of turmoil in the Russian economy on local exchange rates.

Responses to the survey indicate that supply chain issues, complications arising from Russia's disconnection from the SWIFT payment system, and rising prices had the most serious impact on the surveyed firms. Some 50% of respondents assessed the impact of supply chain disruptions due to logistical issues to be serious for their operations, with a further 35% claiming that it had some effect on their operations. The impact of supply chain disruptions on shortages was also notable, with 33% claiming supply chain-linked shortages had a serious effect on operations and a further 44% claiming it had some effect on them. In addition, 33% of firms claimed that Russia's disconnection from the SWIFT payment system had serious affected their business, with another 22% claiming it had some effect on them, testifying to the significant degree of integration of international firms in Central Asia with the Russian economy. However, whilst Russia's disconnection from the SWIFT system had a serious impact on a third of the respondents, it also had no effect on another third of the firms (35%).

Figure 3.3. Firms' reactions to Russia's war and assessment of governmental measures

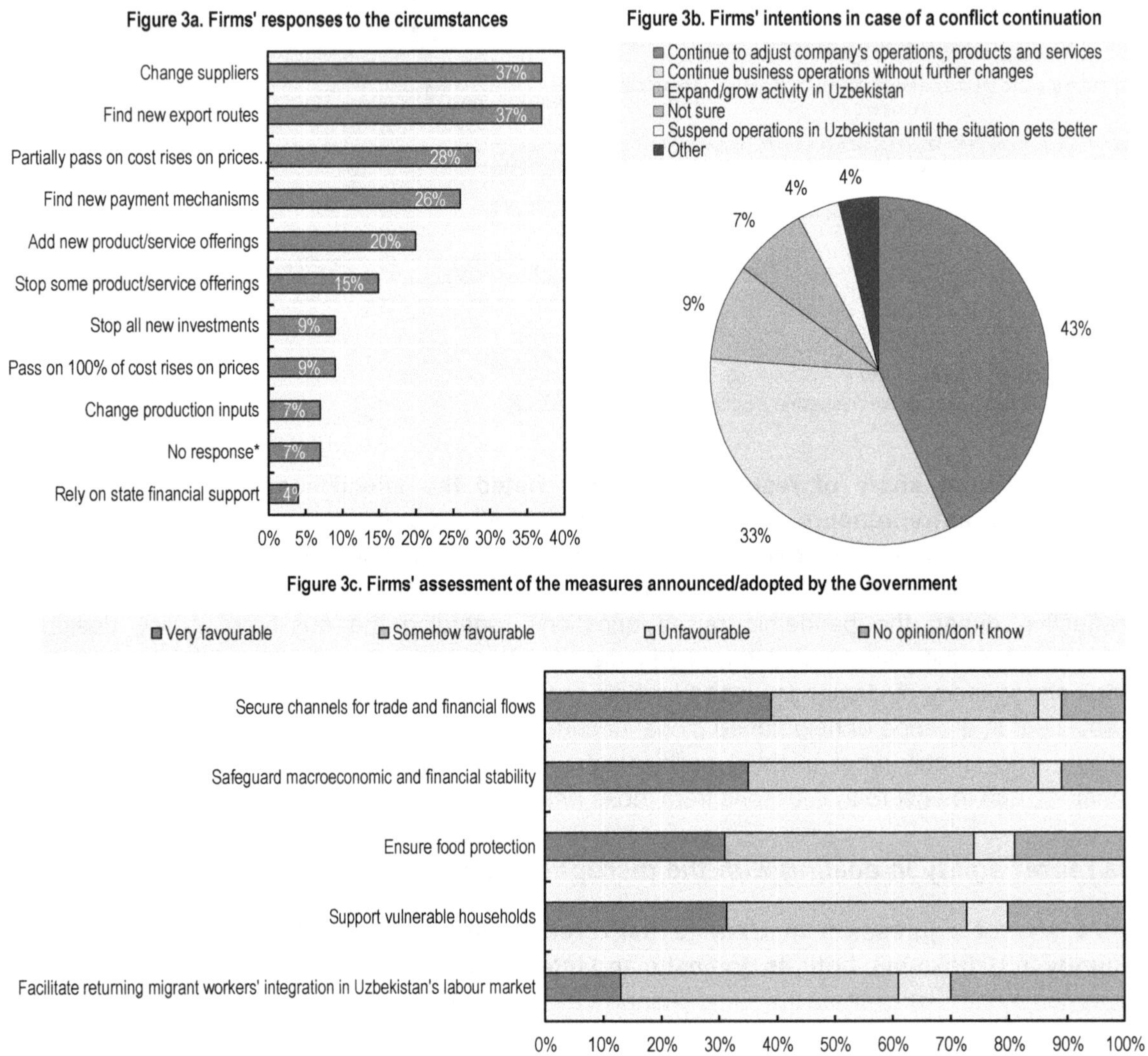

Note: *Because of no business relations with Russia or Ukraine.
Source: EU-OECD Business Climate Assessment Survey in Uzbekistan (2022)

While the share of respondents claiming that price increases for commodities, energy and other non-commodity inputs was serious for their operations was relatively low (30%, 28% and 20% respectively), a majority of firms nevertheless noted that they had been affected by such increases (52%, 41%, and 61%). In other words, only a minority of firms were unaffected by price increases, with it notable that of the three product groups included in the survey, energy price increases were the least likely to have negatively affected the surveyed firms.

The survey respondents outlined a number of possible responses to the challenges posed by Russia's war in Ukraine for Uzbekistan's business community. A significant plurality of respondents demonstrated agility in meeting these challenges, with 37% claiming that they would change suppliers, 37% responding that they would find new export routes, and 26% claiming that they would find new payment mechanisms (Figure 3.3 a). A relatively small number of firms indicated that the crisis would encourage them to innovate, with 20% responding that they planned to add a new product or service offering. At the same time, 28% of respondents noted their intention to pass price increases onto consumer and reduce margins, which may have implications for their ability to reinvest in "the short-to-medium term". Only a small number of respondents indicated their intention to scale back their product offerings (15%), and fewer still to stop investment (9%) or pass on 100% of costs increases (9%).

Respondents appeared committed to the Uzbek market, regardless of whether the war were to continue for another six months from the time of the survey. In such a scenario, only 4% reported that they would suspend operations in the country until the situation improved, while 43% reported that they would adjust their operations to developments as they unfolded and another 33% claimed that they would continue with their current course of action regardless of a prolongation of the war (Figure 3.3 b). An additional 9% of respondents claimed that they would expand their activities in the country should the war continue, though it is not clear whether this was because of the war, or whether pre-existing expansion plans had simply not been derailed.

Firms were generally positive on government measures to support the private sector following Russia's invasion of Ukraine

Interpretation of firms' assessments of interventions from the Uzbek authorities to support the business sector must be qualified by the fact that, unlike the primarily retrospective assessment of the effectiveness of measures to support firms through the COVID-19 pandemic, the impact channels of Russia's war in Ukraine on firms in Ukraine are still being defined, and the full effects remain unclear. Addressing the challenges faced by firms in Uzbekistan that have arisen due to Russia's war will require the government to demonstrate the same agility and creativity as it did during the COVID-19 pandemic, but the policy areas requiring intervention will at times be very different (for example, measures to mitigate disruption in the banking sector, or labour market policies to integrate recent arrivals).

A majority of respondents viewed each all of the surveyed measures taken by the government favourably. The strongest support was for measures to secure trade and financial channels (39% very favourably and 46% somewhat favourably), and for those taken to safeguard macro-economic and financial stability (35% and 50%) (Figure 3.3 c). While these categories are relatively imprecise, and to a certain extent may overlap, they indicate where the perceived needs of European firms' lay following the disruption to the local business climate due to Russia's invasion of Ukraine, and of a general positivity from European firms vis-à-vis the policy direction of the authorities. Firms also positively assessed government measures that were oriented towards social and labour market issues, such as ensuring food protection, supporting vulnerable households, and facilitating the reintegration into the domestic labour market of returning migrants.

Some 67% of respondents considered that the measures implemented by the government to alleviate pressures on the business sector arising from the war were sufficient, while the remaining 33% of respondents suggested an additional range of tax, governance and trade policies for consideration by the authorities. It is difficult to say, however, whether many of the suggested policies are in response to particular challenges faced due to Russia's invasion of Ukraine or respond to broader concerns about the business climate and framework conditions for firms. For example, while issues such as regulatory transparency and non-discriminatory enforcement may be particularly difficult for firms to manage during periods of uncertainty, they are not confined to such periods, but are instead manifestations of long-standing issues in the business climate. Indeed, these issues have been much discussed in OECD work on the business climate in Uzbekistan and Central Asia more broadly, notably in 2021 report (OECD, 2021[1]).

Calls from certain respondents to increase access to non-Russian goods reflect the importance of the Russian market for Uzbek firms, both in terms of finished and intermediate goods. The inability of firms to use Russian suppliers, whether due to sanctions or other logistical difficulties, invariably has an effect on Uzbek firms, but it is not necessarily a weakness of the local business climate so long as firms do not face policy barriers to sourcing inputs from other markets. It does, however, reflect the importance of questions such as infrastructure and trade facilitation as enablers of the local private sector. At the same time, respondents' calls for the elimination of grey imports does suggest inconsistent implementation of customs procedures which could unfairly affect European firms in the country.

References

OECD (2021), *Beyond COVID-19: Prospects for Economic Recovery in Central Asia*, OECD Publishing, Paris, https://www.oecd.org/eurasia/Beyond_COVID%2019_Central%20Asia.pdf. [2]

OECD (2021), *Improving the Legal Environment for Business and Investment in Central Asia*, OECD Publishing, Paris, https://www.oecd.org/eurasia/Improving-LEB-CA-ENG%2020%20April.pdf. [1]

4 Trade facilitation and firm internationalisation in Uzbekistan

Respondents to the survey raised a number of concerns relating to the ease of trade in Uzbekistan. These concerns dovetail with a large body of work the OECD has conducted, in co-operation with the government, on issues around trade facilitation and connectivity. Despite the geographical connectivity penalties Uzbekistan faces due to its double landlocked status, the country has potential to be an attractive destination for market-seeking investment: a large and expanding population, nestled in the midst of a number of other small but potentially high-growth markets. Yet, for both domestic and international firms to harness potential market opportunities, there remains much to be done to lower the cost of trade and raise awareness of external opportunities for the domestic private sector. This chapter introduces a number of insights from the survey, before giving an overview of recent progress, opportunities, and challenges in trade facilitation and export promotion in Uzbekistan.

4.1. Survey observations and overview

A large share of respondents to the survey underscored the importance of market opportunities as a factor in their decisions to enter the country. Some 46% of firms stated that access to the domestic market was one of their main reasons for doing business in the country, indicative of the fact that Uzbekistan's large and fast-growing population and the steady growth in national income are a significant draw for investors. Similarly, over a quarter (27%) of firms emphasised the importance of the regional market in their entry decisions; despite recent disruptions, a third of respondents expected to have seen revenues from domestic trade increase in 2022, while a quarter expected an increase in their international trade. The significance of market-seeking firms is an important one, particularly when contrasted with the fact that access to natural resources (17%) and cheaper labour (10%) appear to have been less important to the surveyed firms.

Nevertheless, there remain a number of issues that limit the market opportunities for local and international firms, both within Uzbekistan and in the broader region. Within Uzbekistan, trade-oriented firms are affected by the same business climate issues as those focussed on the domestic market, such as: weak regulatory enforcement, insufficient competition, and underinvestment in critical connectivity infrastructure. At the same time, firms that have an export-orientation, or which potentially could have, face a number of specific issues: hard and soft infrastructure constraints and broader issues around trade facilitation, a lack of awareness among SMEs of external market opportunities, and an underdevelopment of the export promotion infrastructure necessary to champion Uzbekistan's firms abroad (OECD, 2017[1]; OECD, 2021[2]).

Concerns around these longer-standing trade issues, as well as the impact of recent disruptions to trade, were widely raised in the survey. Some 50% of surveyed firms noted that the war in Ukraine had had a serious impact on supply chains due to logistical challenges, while a further 35% said that they had some impact. A similar picture emerged regarding shortages, with almost half (44%) saying that they had had some kind of effect on their business supply chains due to shortages, with 35% saying shortages had had a serious effect on firm operations.

The impact of recent disruptions on the external aspects of firms' operations in Uzbekistan comes amidst a generally positive, if uneven, appraisal of reforms to support exporting firms. A majority of firms (61%) said that there had been progress over the past five years in improving customs procedures and tariffs, though only 6% said that this progress had been significant. Yet the absolute levels of approval remain low, with 54% of respondents saying that the regulatory framework for customs procedures and tariffs remains weak, and a further 43% rating it as only satisfactory. For exporters, a third of respondents were unable to assess the benefits of the export promotion agency, perhaps indicative of a lack of awareness of its functions and services, or the focus of the surveyed firms on the domestic market. Nevertheless, almost a third (31%) considered the agency to be somewhat useful, and a further 15% very useful. A plurality (41%) of respondents noted that the quality of customs controls were an impediment to the business climate, while respondents also noted a range of areas where improvement could have a significantly positive impact on the business climate, ranging from more support for service exports, elimination of grey imports, and the creation of alternative trade routes.

Supporting export promotion and improving trade connectivity more broadly could bring major benefits to the Uzbek economy, and the market-seeking aspect of respondents' motivations is indicative of certain basic geographical and demographic characteristics that distinguish Uzbekistan from its regional peers. For one, the country is by far the most populous in Central Asia, with its 2021 population of 35 million well above the next most populous country in the region, Kazakhstan, which had a population of 19 million in the same year. The population is less urban than Kazakhstan (58% vs. 50%), but urban population growth is robust (2% in 2021), the country is more densely populated (78 people per square kilometre of land vs. 7 in Kazakhstan), and, with certain historical constraints on internal mobility having recently been lifted it will likely grow more strongly in the years ahead.

The aforementioned reform efforts have already started to have a material impact on Uzbekistan's economy, both in terms of its external sector and the spill-over into the domestic economy. Domestic and international trade have grown substantially since the government of Uzbekistan began its wide-ranging reform programme in 2017, with merchandise trade as a share of GDP having more than doubled between 2016 to the last pre-pandemic year of 2019, from 23.6% of GDP to 59.9% (World Bank, 2023[3]). The expansion of exports has been primarily driven by a large increase in the export of gold, while the export of higher value added and more technologically advanced goods remains low, owing in part to the higher cost of trade and prevailing business climate issues that affect innovation and productivity. Imports have more than doubled between 2010 and 2020, rising from USD 9.2 billion to USD 20 billion (Figure 4.1). Unshackled from previously onerous trading regulations, Uzbekistan's firms have actively been importing new machinery and other capital goods in recent years.

Figure 4.1. Trade decomposition (in value)

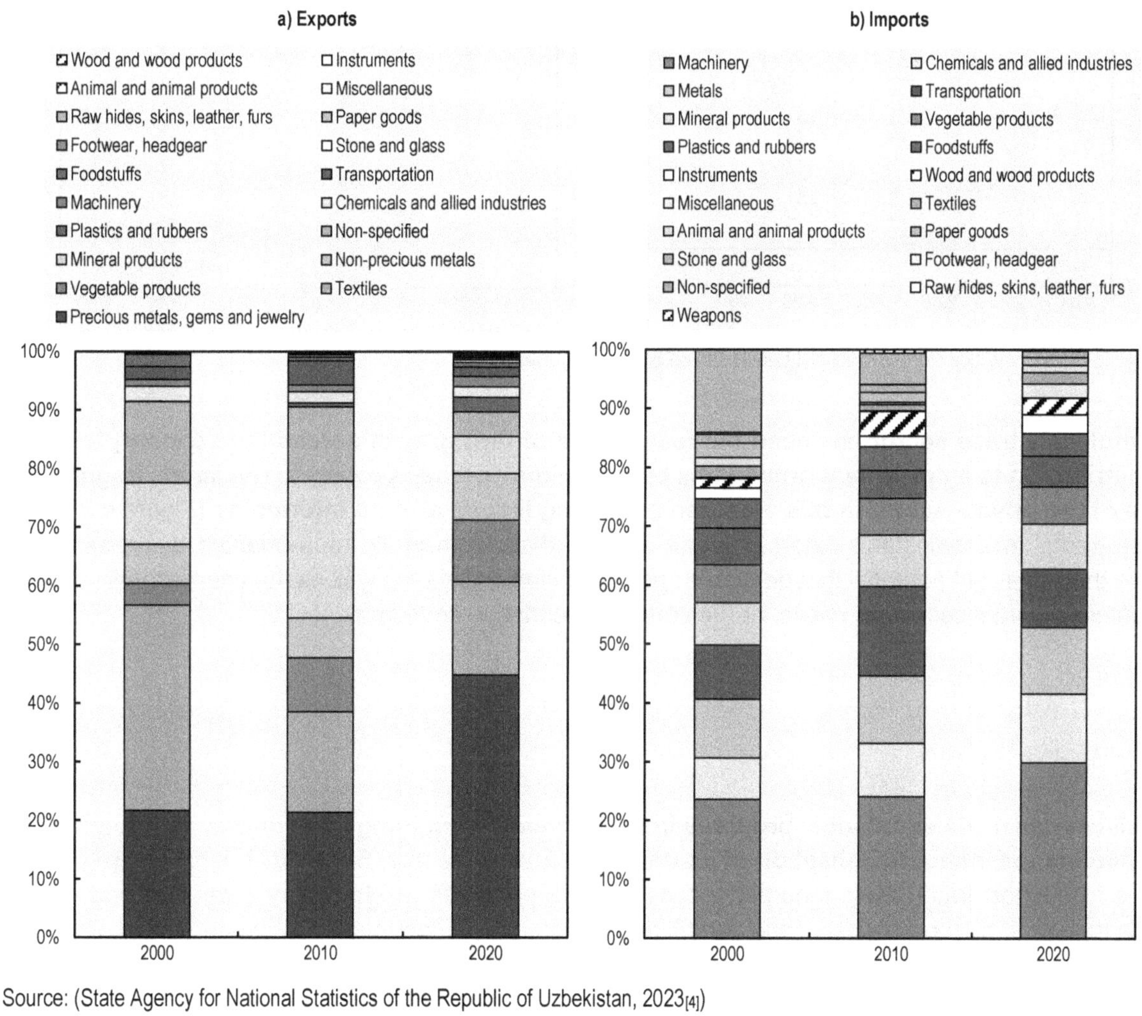

Source: (State Agency for National Statistics of the Republic of Uzbekistan, 2023[4])

Despite significant reserves, Uzbekistan is not a major exporter of natural gas, but its export structure is nevertheless dominated by primary resources. Uzbekistan continues to direct its major natural gas reserves towards the domestic heating and energy sectors as opposed to exporting them, with the country exporting around 25% of gas production and then selling the remainder domestically at below international-market prices (IEA, 2022[5]). The government plans to stop gas exports entirely by 2025, and to use surplus gas for petrochemicals production, which should have a positive impact on the domestic value added of industrial exports (Ibid.). Extractive sectors have been important sources for international currency for the authorities, with the extraction and trade of such primary goods generally the purview of monopolistic SOEs and with transactions directed through the state-managed banking sector. A lack of diversification in exports, and a generally low level of SMEs in international trade, means that Uzbekistan remains largely peripheral to global value chains (GVCs), the integration with which would provide an important source of investment, knowledge and technology transfer (OECD, 2021[2]).

Figure 4.2. Firm dynamism in trade related sectors of the economy

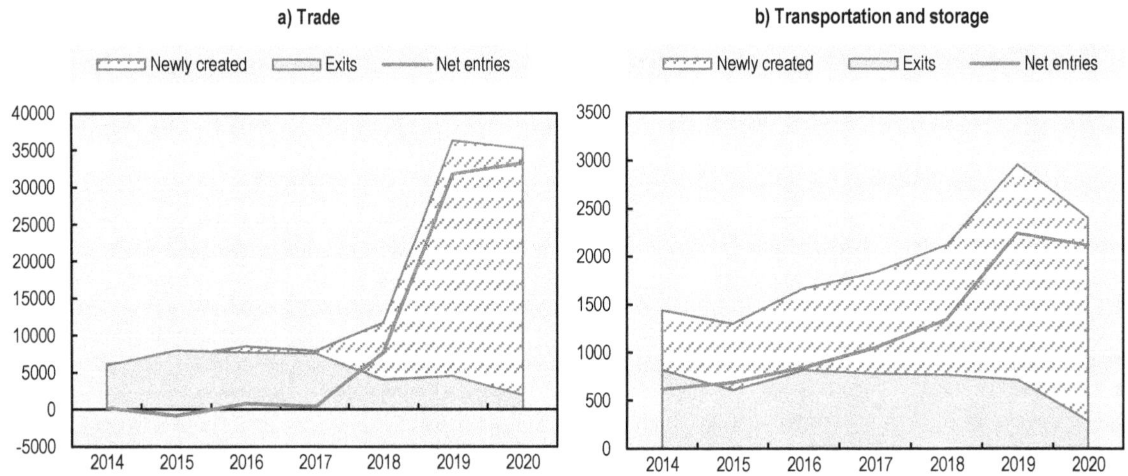

Source: (The State Committee of the Republic of Uzbekistan on Statistics, 2023[6])

The wholesale trade sector has seen the fastest rate of firm growth across the economy, though the contribution to employment growth has been minimal, perhaps owing to the small, fragmented nature of the private sector in this area and prevailing issues around informality (Figure 4.2). The positive trends in Uzbekistan's external sector and the dynamism in its trade-oriented business sector indicate the significant potential that domestic and international trade, as well as the internationalisation of the domestic private sector, can have for the country's economic development

4.2. The government is pursuing a number of regulatory reforms to support firm internationalisation

Uzbekistan has made substantial progress in recent years in opening its economy to foreign trade and enabling the internationalisation of its domestic private sector. Since 2017, legal and regulatory reforms to support trade have generally focussed on three areas: exchange rate reforms and issues relating to foreign currency transactions, tariff liberalisation and issues relating to export restrictions, and, relatedly, integration into the global trade architecture.

4.2.1. Reforms have significantly liberalised exchange rates and currency restrictions

One of the first major reforms undertaken by the current wave of reforms the unification in September 2017 of the multiple exchange rates that had existed up until that point. The government devalued the som by 50%, bringing it in line with the black-market rate that had existed prior to the reform package. In August 2019, the government abolished the limits to the som's daily fluctuations, moving instead to a free float arrangement (OECD, 2019[7]).

At the same time, the government began to liberalise foreign exchange transactions for firms, which had hitherto been highly restricted. The government abandoned the requirement for firms to surrender foreign exchange earnings, immediately easing one of the major blocks on firm growth and reinvestment for both domestic and foreign firms, with this having acted as a *de facto* partial expropriation of foreign earnings (the 'foreign exchange revenue surrender requirements', whereby firms were required to forfeit a part of their export earnings at the official exchange rate).

The exchange rate reforms were accompanied by significant additional reforms relating to the handling of foreign currencies. In addition to the abolition of the surrender requirements, firms were now able to freely purchase foreign currency without restrictions, whether for imports of goods or services, profit repatriation, or other business needs. Similar freedoms were extended to individuals, who from 2017 could purchase foreign currencies for business and travel purposes, and from August 2019 could purchase such currencies with no restrictions.

4.2.2. *A large number of tariffs have been removed*

Throughout 2017-2018, the government began to implement a process of unilateral trade liberalisation, primarily through tariff reductions, reducing import tariffs for around 8,000 out of 10,800 items, of which around 5,000 were removed entirely (World Bank, 2021[8]). The reduction of tariffs had the effect of lowering effective tariff rates from 14.9% in September 2017 to around 7.5% in 2020 (Ibid).

In addition to lowering most peak tariffs, reforms moved the remaining tariffs from mixed and compound tariffs to a more transparent system of ad-valorem tariffs, and removed most discriminatory excise taxes on certain imports (World Bank, 2021[8]). At the same time, the government also lifted export bans on flour, rice, meat, and vegetable oil, while a green corridor for simplified customs procedures was implemented for the export of fruit and vegetables to a number of key markets, notably Russia, Kazakhstan and the Kyrgyz Republic. Taken together, these reforms have helped make Uzbekistan's trade more competitive, as attested to by the rapid growth of merchandise trade since 2017.

4.2.3. *Uzbekistan has reignited its engagement with the global trade architecture*

Discussions on WTO membership resumed in 2020, some 15 years after the last formal meeting on the country's accession (World Bank, 2021[8]). Since then, the government has prepared a roadmap for accession, submitted an updated *Memorandum on the Foreign Trade Regime,* something which marks a crucial step in resuming accession negotiations, and included achieving WTO membership as a stated aim of the government's 2022 *Development Strategy of New Uzbekistan for 2022-2026* (Republic of Uzbekistan, 2022[9]). Should Uzbekistan be successful in implementing the necessary WTO principles for accession, the country is likely to see a significant reduction in the costs, time, and uncertainties that continue to characterise the existing regulatory framework for foreign trade (World Bank, 2021[8]).

Co-operation between the EU and Uzbekistan on trade issues has also intensified in recent years. In July 2018, the Council of Europe adopted directives to negotiate an Enhanced Partnership and Co-operation Agreement (EPCA), an upgraded version of the Partnership and Co-operation Agreement in force since 1999. The EPCA was concluded in February 2021, and Uzbekistan then obtained the aforementioned GSP+ status in April 2021. This status allows Uzbekistan to benefit from the basic GSP system (permitting the export of 3,000 goods to the EU without customs duties, and 3,200 goods at reduced rates), and grants Uzbek producers and exporters unilateral preferences when exporting to the European market, such as a doubling of duty-free exports (OECD, 2021[2]).

4.3. Uzbekistan has simplified its trade facilitation framework, though a number of barriers remain

The government has undoubtedly made progress in removing barriers to trade. Nevertheless, there remain a number of issues relating to trade facilitation – i.e., the ease in fulfilling the logistical and procedural requirements necessary for importing and exporting – that continue to weigh heavily on the business climate. Addressing these issues is a policy goal of the government, and success in doing so would have a significant and positive impact on the ability of Uzbekistan to expand and diversify its trade.

Issues that fall into the category of trade facilitation can affect firms in a number of ways. By virtue of being double-landlocked, Uzbekistan's traders already suffer from a geographical connectivity penalty, one which is also felt by international firms who may seek to expand into the market (ITF, 2019[10]). As discussed in a, much of the cost for traders in the region is incurred through soft infrastructure problems, in contrast to the hard, physical infrastructure to which policy attention can often gravitate. The implication is that higher costs involved in moving goods and services across borders, compounded by a high degree of uncertainty in the time and processes involved in doing so, can either discourage firms from exporting or importing, or, once the cost is factored in, render their exports uncompetitive on external markets.

Box 4.1. The OECD Trade Facilitation Indicators

To help governments improve their border procedures, reduce trade costs, boost trade flows and reap greater benefits from international trade, the OECD has developed a set of Trade Facilitation Indicators (TFIs) that identify areas for action and enable the potential impact of trade facilitation reforms to be assessed. The OECD TFIs help track the specific areas where progress has been made on the implementation of the TFA, as well as other trade facilitation policies. The TFIs also help identify where further reforms are needed.

Their key value added is in identifying changes in both the regulatory frameworks for trade facilitation measures and their implementation in practice. The indicators thus cover the full spectrum of border procedures for more than 160 economies across different income levels, geographical regions, and levels of development. The TFIs take values from 0 to 2, where 2 designates the best performance that can be achieved.

OECD TFIs: Overview of key dimensions and measures

Indicator	Key components
(a) Information availability	▪ publication of customs and trade-related regulations and information, including through webpages on the Internet ▪ the existence and functioning of enquiry points ▪ specific functions for businesses (dedicated webpages/portals, manuals etc.)
(b) Involvement of the trade community (Consultations)	▪ structures for consultations ▪ established guidelines for consultations ▪ publications of drafts ▪ existence of notice-and-comment frameworks
(c) Advance rulings	▪ prior statements by the administration to requesting traders concerning the classification, origin, valuation method, etc., applied to specific goods at the time of importation ▪ the rules and process applied to such statements
(d) Appeal procedures	▪ the possibility and modalities to appeal administrative decisions by border agencies
(e) Fees and charges	▪ disciplines on the fees and charges imposed on imports and exports ▪ disciplines on penalties
(f) Formalities – documents	▪ acceptance of copies ▪ simplification of trade documents ▪ harmonisation in accordance with international standards
(g) Formalities – automation	▪ electronic exchange of data ▪ use of automated risk management ▪ automated border procedures
(h) Formalities – procedures	▪ streamlining of border controls (inspections, clearance) ▪ separation of release for clearance ▪ single submission points for all required documentation (single windows) ▪ post-clearance audits ▪ the existence and functioning of Authorised Operators (AOs) programmes
(i) Border agency co-operation - internal	▪ control delegation to customs authorities ▪ co-operation between various border agencies of the country
(j) Border agency co-operation - external	▪ co-operation with neighbouring and third countries
(k) Governance and impartiality	▪ transparency of customs structures and functions ▪ accountability and ethics policy

In 2022, the OECD reassessed Uzbekistan's performance in the OECD Trade Facilitation Indicators (TFIs) (Box 4.1), the country's first update since 2019, two years into the ongoing reform process (OECD, Forthcoming). At that point, the country had already begun to make progress from the earlier benchmarking, particularly in the areas of procedural formalities and the involvement of the international trade community. Since that point, the country has continued to improve its general performance, with the most significant progress being made in the areas of availability of trade-related information, the involvement of the trade community, simplification and streamlining of fees and charges, simplification and harmonisation of trade-related documents, and domestic and cross-border agency co-operation (Figure 4.3). In contrast, limited progress has been made with respect to advance rulings, appeal procedures and the automation of border procedures.

Figure 4.3. Uzbekistan in the OECD Trade Facilitation Indicators, 2017-2022

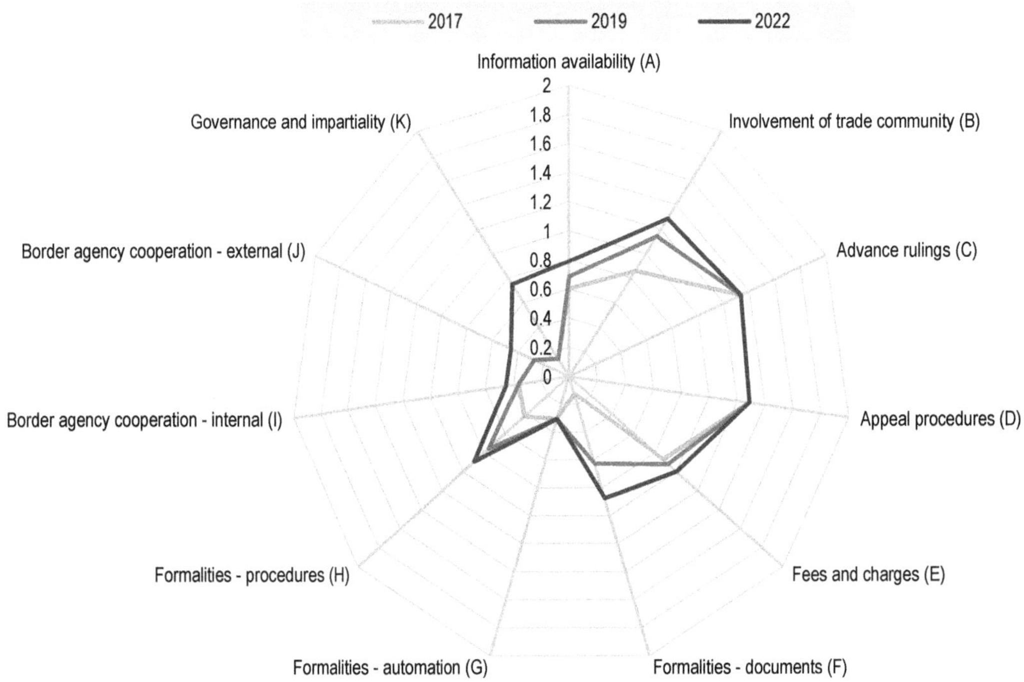

Source: (OECD, 2023[11])

The performance of Uzbekistan in the TFIs is broadly in line with the average performance for lower-middle income economies (LMICs) in a number of areas. This includes transparency and predictability (the latter includes aspects such as the involvement of the trade community and advance rulings, and appeal procedures) (Figure 4.4). A comparison with the LMIC group also highlights a number of more challenging areas, such as information availability, fees and charges, simplification and harmonisation of trade-related documents, automation of border processes, and co-operation with border agencies. While progress has been made, Uzbekistan lags the LMIC group on most of these areas, and significantly lags the OECD average.

Figure 4.4. Trade facilitation in international comparison, 2022

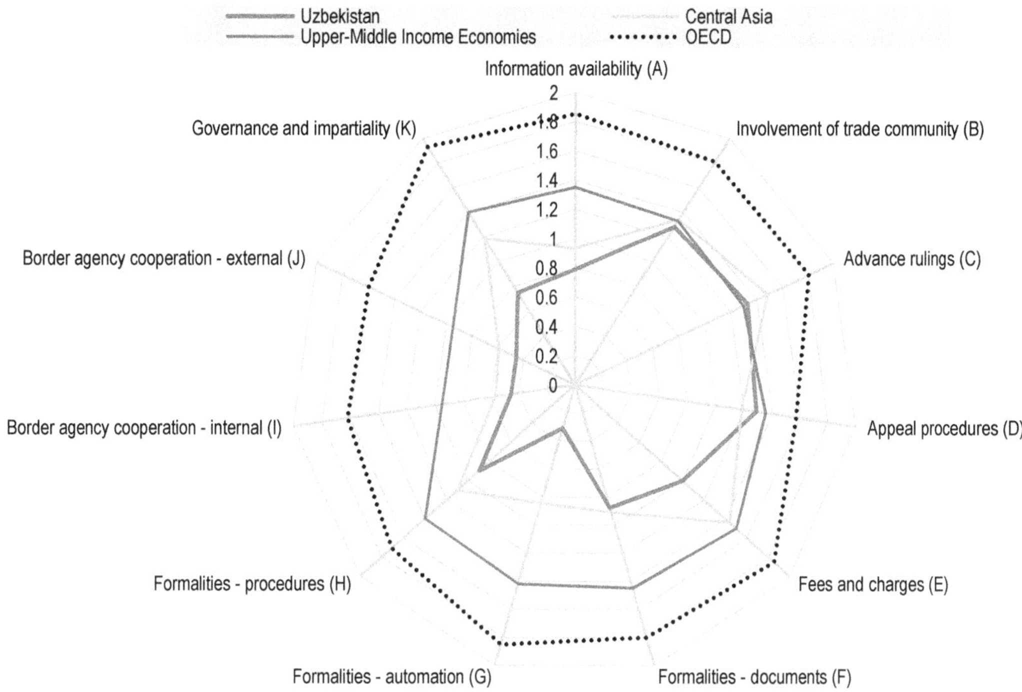

Source: (OECD, 2023[11])

In a 2023, the OECD noted a number of notable improvements due to recent policy reforms, as well as certain areas where additional improvement could meaningfully improve the local business climate (OECD, Forthcoming[12]). By increasing the user-friendliness of information concerning the rate of duties, export and import procedures, and general trade-relevant legislation, information on trade agreements and by providing user manuals on how new border systems would work, the government has markedly improved transparency for trading firms. Progress was also made in improving the inclusion of a new and broader array of stakeholders in consultation processes on trade-related policy changes, while progress has also been made through the introduction of an advance rulings system as well as the introduction of procedural rules for appeals on trade-related matters. Work in all of these areas has helped improve transparency and predictability for traders in and with the country.

The government has also made progress in streamlining border processes, this being achieved through the establishment of a Single Window for trade, of Post-Clearance Audits, and of an Authorised Operators (AOs) programme. These changes have been added to with new procedures for the treatment of perishable goods and their treatment in customs clearance, pre-shipment inspections, the use of customs brokers, and the temporary admission of goods. The streamlining of border processes has also been improved by the simplification and harmonisation of trade-related documents and the automation of procedures, with Uzbekistan having made particular progress in the introduction of electronic payment possibilities of duties, automated risk management, the acceptance of copies and the use of international standards.

The government also has taken steps towards strengthening inter-agency mechanisms in support of border agency co-operation, with co-operation, coordination, information exchange and assistance now involving all domestic agencies that are involved in cross-border trade. There are now regular meetings between the different public agencies involved in the procedures required to import or export goods, supplemented by informal and ad hoc coordination mechanisms between agencies to address particular events at the border. Importantly, national legislation now allows for cross-border co-operation, coordination, information exchange and mutual assistance with border authorities in neighbouring countries.

Assessments by the OECD on Uzbekistan's performance also highlighted a number of areas for improvement, which largely dovetail with observations in the survey and other OECD work on trade facilitation and connectivity in the region. For example, in a context of continuous disruptions, the need for transparency and predictability takes on additional importance, since it can support firms by providing early warnings and help build supply chain resilience. As noted above, Uzbekistan has made progress in this area, but there is much more that can be done in terms of increasing the availability and comprehensiveness of information online.

The OECD also noted the need for improvement in a number of areas. This included further simplifying trade documentation (for example, by increasing the share of supporting documents for which copies are accepted), automating border processes (for example, increasing the share of import and export procedures that can be processed electronically, or allowing advance electronic payment for duties and taxes), and streamlining border processes (for example, by finalising the introduction of an automated risk management system for customs and other agencies involved in cross-border trade). Enhancing border agency co-operation – for example by introducing an institutionalised mechanism for supporting inter-agency coordination, or introducing the possibility of government agencies to delegate controls to another agency – was also highlighted as key areas for improvement.

4.4. Additional targeted support could help SMEs access foreign markets

Demand-side issues to trade, such as the awareness of external opportunities and raising firm capacities to navigate customs procedures, are also important for firm internationalisation. Helping firms – specifically SMEs – in Uzbekistan to internationalise was a key motivation of the government and the OECD when it undertook a 2017 peer review of the country's export promotion policies to support firm internationalisation, a report that was further developed in 2021-22 through a monitoring exercise (OECD, 2017[1]; OECD, 2021[2]).

SMEs play a significant role in creating growth and employment in Uzbekistan, accounting for 55% GDP and 75% of formal employment in 2020. Their contribution to exports, however, remains limited, suggesting that barriers to exporting continue to mitigate their potential contribution to growth. In the last pre-pandemic year of 2019, SMEs generated 27% of exports, with the share falling to 20.5% in 2020. These figures reflect direct exports, that is, they omit the indirect exports to which SMEs contribute through their integration into global value chains (GVCs) and their roles in the broader industrial ecosystems of larger firms in the country. The inclusion of Uzbekistan in OECD databases such as the Trade in Value Added (TiVA) database would make it easier to capture the broader role of Uzbekistan's SMEs in its export-orientated industries.

In the face of the connectivity penalties faced by Uzbekistan and the relatively high cost of international trade, the country's SMEs generally remain oriented towards the domestic market or immediate regional neighbours, particularly in the trade and manufacturing sectors. Targeted support programmes to increase SMEs' knowledge of new export opportunities, and to help them to navigate the procedures necessary to access them, has become a key area of policy activity in recent years.

After undertaking its initial peer review of Uzbekistan's export promotion policies in 2017, the OECD made a number of recommendations to the government Many of these recommendations remain relevant, including the following:

- developing consulting activities to improve SMEs' knowledge of foreign markets, including export market potential and product certification requirements and opportunities;
- expanding the export-promotion network abroad and providing a clear branding strategy in target markets in co-operation with the business community: and
- monitoring the work and impact of export institutions to allocate resources more effectively using key performance indicators and comprehensive evaluation strategies across different institutions.

Since these recommendations were made in 2017, Uzbekistan has made significant progress in a number of areas. Several export promotion institutions have been developed in the intervening period, including the Export Promotion Agency (EPA), which was established under the Ministry of Investments and Foreign Trade (MIFT). The establishment of the EPA allowed the government to consolidate and rationalise the mandates of several pre-existing institutions, including the Small Business and Entrepreneurship Development Agency under the Cabinet of Ministers. Since its establishment, the EPA has become a key actor in the export promotion landscape, helping SMEs to access trade-related finance, engaging with authorities and negotiating export contracts. It also provides information on export markets to the country's SMEs, in collaboration with research centres like the Centre for Economic Research and Reform (CERR) and the Centre for Research on Sectoral Markets and Productivity in Manufacturing. The agency also has the important role of overseeing and implementing the *Made in Uzbekistan* promotional brand.

The government has also deepened its co-operation with the private sector as it seeks to expand the internationalisation of the private sector. One important area of work in this regard has been work to support SMEs with standardisation and quality infrastructure, for example efforts by the Agency for Technical Regulation to provide exporting business with support on certification issues. The EPA has also sought to address knowledge and skills gaps that may prevent SMEs from exporting by establishing consulting and marketing services, with these now a crucial element of its mandate. The EPA has six thematic divisions, of which two are dedicate to export market research and analysis.

Nevertheless, there remain a number of areas where additional policy intervention could markedly improve the capacities of Uzbek SMEs to internationalise. The supply, for example, of certification services could be increased and made more accessible. As noted in the monitoring note in 2021, the EPA could provide cost-sharing options for these and other services in order to broaden the scope of SMEs that can access them. Partnerships with international certification bodies and companies could also improve the 'quality infrastructure' knowledge necessary for Uzbekistan's SMEs to make the most of opportunities that have emerged through GSP+ and which may emerge through further WTO harmonisation.

The *Made in Uzbekistan* brand was an important step in creating a recognisable identity for Uzbekistan in potential export markets, but work still has to be done to associate Uzbek SMEs with a clear value proposition. This is an area where the network of the EPA abroad, particularly through embassies and trade houses, could be used more strategically.

References

IEA (2022), *Uzbekistan 2022: Energy Policy Review*, International Energy Agency, Paris, https://iea.blob.core.windows.net/assets/0d00581c-dc3c-466f-b0c8-97d25112a6e0/Uzbekistan2022.pdf. [5]

ITF (2019), *Enhancing Connectivity and Freight in Central Asia*, OECD Publishing, Paris, https://www.itf-oecd.org/sites/default/files/docs/connectivity-freight-central-asia_2.pdf. [10]

OECD (2023), *Uzbekistan*, OECD Trade Facilitation Indicators, OECD Publishing, Paris, https://www.oecd.org/trade/topics/trade-facilitation/. [11]

OECD (2021), *Beyond COVID-19: Prospects for Economic Recovery in Central Asia*, OECD Publishing, Paris, https://www.oecd.org/eurasia/Beyond_COVID%2019_Central%20Asia.pdf. [14]

OECD (2021), *Boosting the Internationalisation of Firms through better Export Promotion Policies in Uzbekistan*, OECD Eurasia Policy Insights, OECD Publishing, Paris, https://www.oecd.org/eurasia/Monitoring_Review_Uzbekistan_ENG.pdf. [2]

OECD (2020), *COVID-19 Crisis Response in Central Asia*, OECD Publishing, Paris, https://read.oecd-ilibrary.org/view/?ref=129_129634-ujyjsqu30i&title=COVID-19-crisis-response-in-central-asia. [13]

OECD (2019), *Improving the Legal Environment for Business and Investment in Central Asia*, OECD Publishing, Paris, https://www.oecd.org/eurasia/Improving-LEB-CA-ENG%2020%20April.pdf. [7]

OECD (2017), *Boosting SME Internationalisation in Uzbekistan through better Export Promotion Policies*, OECD Publishing, Paris, https://www.oecd.org/eurasia/competitiveness-programme/central-asia/Uzbekistan_Peer_review_note_dec2017_final.pdf. [1]

OECD (Forthcoming), *Enhancing Trade Connectivity in Central Asia*, OECD Publishing, Paris. [12]

Republic of Uzbekistan (2022), *Development Strategy of New Uzbekistan for 2022-2026*, https://uzembassy.kz/upload/userfiles/files/Development%20Strategy%20of%20Uzbekistan.pdf. [9]

State Agency for National Statistics of the Republic of Uzbekistan (2023), *External Economic Statistics*, State Agency for National Statistics, Tashkent, https://stat.uz/ru/ofitsialnaya-statistika/merchandise-trade. [4]

The State Committee of the Republic of Uzbekistan on Statistics (2023), *Small Business and Entrepreneurship*, The State Committee of the Republic of Uzbekistan on Statistics, Tashkent, https://stat.uz/en/official-statistics/small-business-and-entrepreneurship. [6]

World Bank (2023), *World Bank Development Indicators*, World Bank, DC, https://databank.worldbank.org/source/world-development-indicators. [3]

World Bank (2021), *Assessing Uzbekistan's Transition: Country Economic Memorandum*, World Bank, DC, https://documents1.worldbank.org/curated/en/862261637233938240/pdf/Full-Report.pdf. [8]

5 Transforming the legal and regulatory environment for business in Uzbekistan

Responses to the survey suggest that firms consider ongoing legal and regulatory reforms to support the business climate in Uzbekistan to be moving in the right direction. At the same time, respondents note that there remains significant work to be done both on the implementation of these reforms, and on additional and complementary pro-competition reforms. These views are in line with OECD analysis on a number of areas highlighted by respondents, such as overall framework conditions for business, taxation, and competition policy. While the legal and regulatory environment for business in Uzbekistan has improved significantly developed since 2017, reducing many unnecessary fixed costs of doing business, the survey highlights a number of areas where more work is necessary to foster private sector development.

5.1. Survey observations and overview

Responses to the survey reveal a mixed picture of how firms in Uzbekistan regard the speed, effectiveness and direction of ongoing reforms to support private sector development. For example, respondents overwhelming reported that Uzbekistan had a business-friendly climate, with 28% reporting that it was very friendly, and 54% reporting that it was somewhat friendly. Only 9% of respondents claimed that the business climate was not friendly. Yet this generally positive assessment belies a significantly more mixed appraisal of various local indicators of the health of the country's business climate.

For example, a significant proportion of firms reported that business registration and licensing, labour legislation and migration policy were satisfactory, though significantly fewer rated these indicators as strong. This is perhaps unsurprising, given that these are areas where the government is continuing to implement reforms, and it is notable that a majority of respondents agreed that in each of these areas, the government had made some or major progress over the previous five years (Figure 5.1 b). Improvements to the registration and licensing requirements for firms was were among the key areas for action highlighted OECD *Improving the Legal Environment for Business* report, together with tax policy, another area where a significant majority of respondents report some or major progress, even if relatively few rate the current tax administration and policy as strong (OECD, 2021[1]).

Figure 5.1. Firm-level evaluation of reforms and recent progress in Uzbekistan

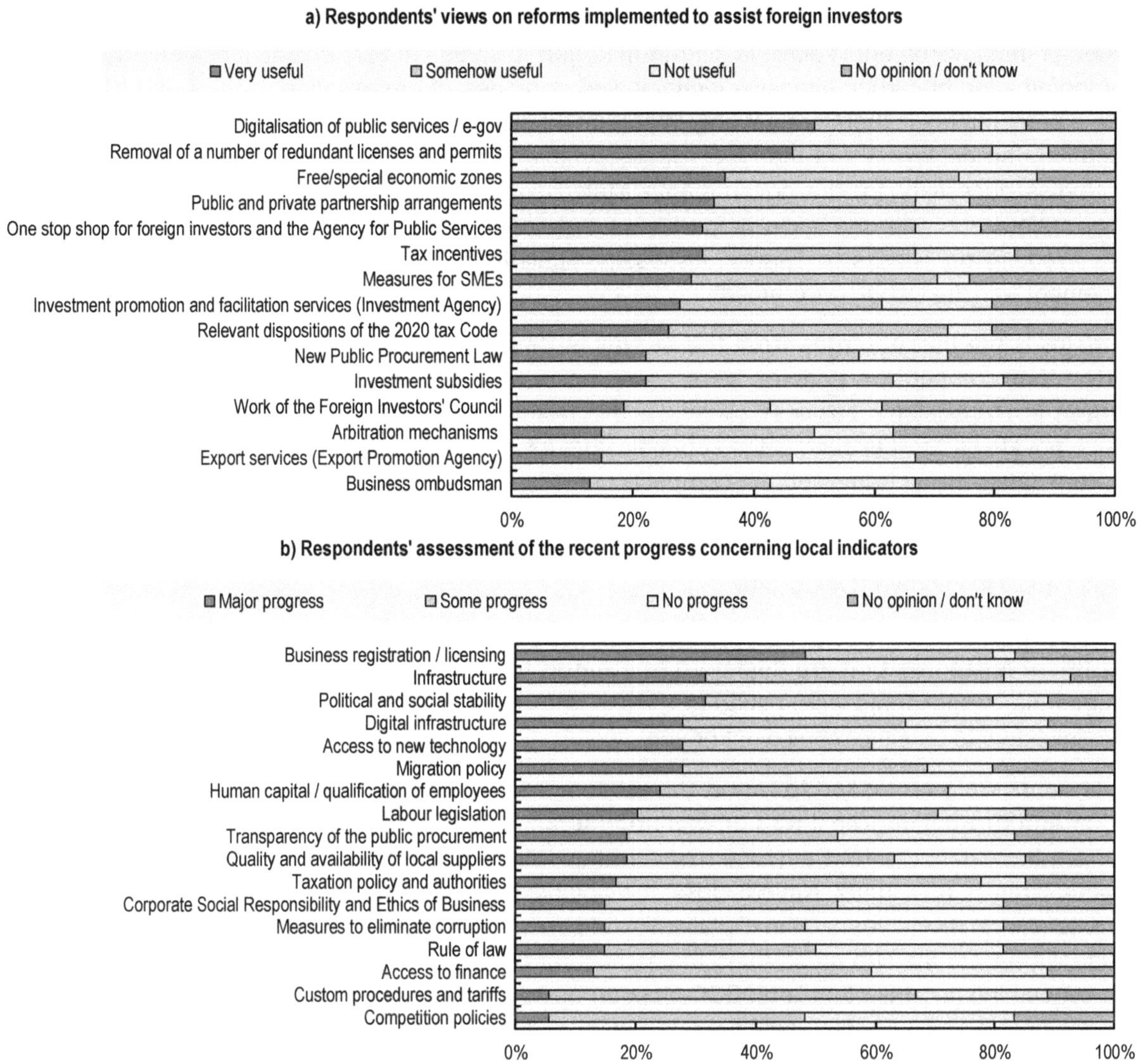

Note: As a percent of the total number of respondents.
Source: EU-OECD Business Climate Assessment Survey in Uzbekistan (2022)

At the same time, 50% or more of respondents rated over half the indicators as weak, a significantly larger proportion than the corresponding figure for strong, the highest figures for which were 20% (political and social stability) and 19% (business registration and licensing). The percentage of firms to rate the remaining 15 indicators as strong was less than 10%. Nevertheless, it is encouraging to note that a sizable plurality – and in many cases a majority – of firms assessed the progress of the government's reforms in each area to be positive, which perhaps underscores the generally positive overall assessment offered by respondents.

5.1.1. Transparency and competition remain problematic areas for firms

A number of business climate issues emerged as particularly problematic through firms' responses to the survey, each reflecting long-standing issues in the legal and regulatory environment. Transparency of public procurement remains a significant challenge for firms, with 56% respondents reporting this as weak, and only 2% reporting it was strong. This is an issue not just for

European firms, but for the broader private sector, and indeed the public sector, which through its significant purchasing power is able, for example, to privilege low-carbon and sustainable technologies and solutions through procurement. The reverse is also true – poor procurement decisions now may make it harder for the government to achieve long-term targets such as net zero should those decisions result in the grandfathering of carbon intensive technologies or modes of organisation. Addressing transparency issues in procurement is therefore not only important for increasing the opportunities for firms, but also for accelerating the deployment of the types of sustainable and productivity-enhancing infrastructures and technologies necessary for the government's stated socio-economic ambitions. Access to finance is another major issue, with the same proportion of respondents reporting that it is strong (2%) and weak (56%). Working on access to finance issues, particularly for SMEs, remains a key pillar of OECD engagement with the Uzbek government.

One major issue that emerges from the survey is that of competition. While 56% of respondents reported that competition policies were weak, none reported that they were strong. This is a key weakness in Uzbekistan's business climate and a major barrier to the development of a resilient and inclusive private sector. On each of the sub-indicators for competition policy, a majority reported that they were weak (institutional framework for competition policy – 52%; concentration control – 54%; measures in place against cartels and concerted practices – 57%; control of market dominance and monopoly practices – 67%). This is an issue about which the authorities are aware, and on which they are working with the OECD to improve (OECD, 2022[2]).

As representatives of European businesses in Uzbekistan, firms were also asked to assess government measures that are designed to support foreign investors (Figure 5.1), For 11 of the 15 measures that respondents were asked to assess, a majority considered government efforts to support foreign investors to be either somewhat or very useful.

Respondents were not asked to report the relative importance of each measure, simply to answer whether and to what degree it was or was not useful. It therefore is not possible to determine from the responses the extent to which any one measure has affected investment decisions taken – or not – by European firms in the country. Nevertheless, it is notable that two areas where government reforms have been extensive in recent years – the digitalisation of public services and the removal of redundant licenses and permits – were the two areas rated the highest for being 'very' useful (50% and 46% respectively), which echoes the findings of earlier OECD work on these areas. A significant plurality of firms responded they were unable to assess the usefulness of a number of measures, perhaps due to a lack of awareness of these among the European business community.

In many ways, the responses to the survey align with the OECD's own analysis of the business climate in Uzbekistan. That there has been major progress in improving the business climate is clear, notably through the market liberalisation reforms discussed in Chapter 4, as well as through numerous reforms to the legal and regulatory environment for entrepreneurship and investment (OECD, 2021[1]). At the same time, the impact of these reforms on the *de facto* operational environment for firms remains limited, in large part due to only piecemeal progress in implementing reforms that address competition, investment and development in certain key framework conditions for business, and in consistently implementing the *de jure* changes to the regulatory environment.

5.2. The government is undertaking a wide-ranging set of regulatory reforms to support private sector development and foreign investors

Since beginning a sweeping set of reforms in 2017, Uzbekistan has made significant steps towards improving the legal and regulatory environment for business. Activity has been intense on the part of policymakers and regulators, and in recent years there has been a large volume of new legislation that affects, directly or indirectly, private enterprise in the country. Many recent legislative changes have addressed long-standing uncertainties and weaknesses in the legal and regulatory environment for business, notably the 2020 *Law on Investment and Investment Activities* and the substantially revised 2020 tax code, while an entrepreneurial code, which will condense numerous hitherto disparate pieces of business-related legislation into one law, was drafted in 2022.

At the same time, in 2017-2022, much of the government's policy focus was on what might be described as the low-hanging fruit of reform. Certain notable barriers to business were certainly addressed – it is, for example, significantly simpler and cheaper to start a business – but other barriers, often related to inveterately difficult policy and political economy issues, remain either in place or only partially alleviated.

5.2.1. A number of high-level strategies guide the reform process

A number of high-level strategy documents guide the reform process. The guiding strategic document for the initial stages of the reform process was the *National Development Strategy for 2017-21* (NDS), which set out the government's plans to liberalise the economy, reduce the role of the state, strengthen governance and increase the role of the private sector and foreign investment (Republic of Uzbekistan, 2017[3]). The NDS was supplemented by the operational *2019-21 Reform Roadmap*, (Republic of Uzbekistan, 2019[4]). Both documents and a large number of presidential decrees, laws and bylaws, are indicative of the breadth and depth of the reform agenda. In 2022, the NDS was replaced by the *National Development Strategy for 2022-2026*, which builds on the priorities of the earlier document and adds a number of specific targets: a 1.6-fold increase in GDP per capita by the end of the project period, per capita income to reach USD 4,000 by 2030, reducing annual inflation to 5% by 2023, increasing the volume of industrial production by 40% and increasing the share of industry in GDP, and achieving a number of targets around climate change and sustainability, electricity generation, and WTO accession.

To support the implementation its private sector and business climate development priorities, the government has undertaken significant institutional reform. It has created new institutions and agencies, reformed existing ones, and increased the autonomy of certain existing institutions. These reorganisations represent a concerted effort to ensure that relevant institutions are empowered and able to implement the government's reform agenda, as well as being representative of the general trend in downsizing and streamlining the public administration. A number of such developments are detailed below:

- The government established the Strategic Reforms Agency (SRA), under the president's office, which both oversees and evaluates ongoing reforms whilst also being tasked with formulating additional possibilities for policy change and reform.
- The government established the Ministry of Investment, Industry and Trade (MIIT) and the Ministry of Economy and Finance (MEF), with these being tasked to improve the overall business and investment climate.
- To support privatisation, the government established the State Assets Management Agency (SAMA), which replaced the now-dissolved State Committee on Privatisation, Demonopolisation and the Development of Competition.
- The government also created the Capital Markets Development Agency (CAMA), which is working with SAMA on its privatisation strategy as well as independently on establishing a functioning capital market in Uzbekistan.
- The government also created the Agency for the Development of Small Businesses and Entrepreneurs under the MEPR, with the MEPR also responsible for non-agricultural land reforms and the development of the country's urbanisation strategy.
- The government also established a new body to co-ordinate a horizontal approach for the development, coordination and implementation of anti-corruption policy through interdepartmental

commissions at the national level (Republican Inter-Agency Commission), and across the country's regions (territorial inter-agency commissions).

- A business ombudsman has been created under the aegis of the Presidential Administration.

In 2022, the government drafted a new Entrepreneurial Code (EC), which consolidates a number of hitherto disparate pieces of business-related legislation. The current draft EC includes key sections that are organised in line with international standards, including clear definitions of: businesses, in particular of SMEs with associated thresholds and a time-bound reference period, as well as a clear distinction between the definition and purpose of business entities and social enterprises; their rights and obligations; the provisions needed for a sound regulatory framework for businesses, in particular the definition of the procedure for business registration and closure, an important step for enterprise formalisation; and, the rules concerning the nature and modalities of state support to businesses. In addition, the document spells out a hierarchy of normative acts between international treaties and national laws, as it gives primacy to international treaties ratified by Uzbekistan over the EC, and primacy of the EC over all other legal acts related to entrepreneurship (current Article 2).

5.2.2. Regulatory reforms have significantly simplified business registration and licensing

Opening a business has become far easier. The registration process for domestic entrepreneurs has been significantly improved, with a shift towards online registration and the use of digital platforms (World Bank, 2019[5]). Businesses can register physically at one of the Public Service Centres, located in Tashkent and with branches in each region, or through the online registration platform www.fo.birdacha.uz. Minimum capital requirements for establishing a Joint Stock Company (JSC) or a Limited Liability Company (LLC) were abolished in March 2019 to establish (Dentons, 2019[6]). Renewal procedures every three years involving an apostille could also be discontinued.

The licenses and permits needed for running a business continue to be streamlined. In April 2018, the two presidential decrees –"On Measures to Further Reduce and Simplify Licensing and Licensing Procedures in the Field of Entrepreneurial Activity" and "On Improving Business Conditions" acknowledged that many licenses and permits did not meet modern standards and had become obsolete. Moreover, they recognised that the process of license issuance was too slow and that government bodies' interaction remained too limited. The decrees called for reducing the number of activities requiring a license and the time required to obtain licenses, removing time limits on most licenses, and authorising applicants to carry out licensed activities if the public authorities failed to meet the established deadlines for processing licence applications (Republic of Uzbekistan, 2018[7]).

5.2.3. The government is continuing reforms to the tax adminsitration

Since 2017, the government has been reforming the tax system, with changes intended to simplify tax policy and administration. Starting in 2018, personal and corporate taxes, for all firms of all sizes, were unified at a flat rate of 12%; firm size classifications changed from being employee-based to turnover-based, and a new unified rate of tax for small firms was introduced at 4% of turnover (World Bank, 2021[8]). Rules were also changed to allow small firms to pay VAT, which in turn has allowed them to operate more efficiently in the VAT supply chain to larger firms – something that has been identified as a barrier to SME growth (OECD, 2021[1]). The new code was introduced in January 2020, and its introduction follows a major overhaul of the country's tax system (Republic of Uzbekistan, 2019[9]). Despite the impact of the COVID-19 pandemic, tax revenues increased from 19.2% of GDP in 2019 to 19.5% of GDP in 2020, due in part to an increase of the tax base and increased employment formalisation offsetting revenue loss from lower tax rates (World Bank, 2021[8]).

5.2.4. *The government's privatisation programme has accelerated in recent years*

To address the role of the state in the economy, the government has begun to implement a broad programme of corporatisation as it prepares for the privatisation of a number of state-owned enterprises (SOEs) (Republic of Uzbekistan, 2018[10]). One of the fundamental challenges for policy-makers and investors in understanding the extent of the state's presence in the economy is a question of measurement and classification, with legislation classifying only 100% state-owned state-unitary enterprises as SOEs (Republic of Uzbekistan, 2006[11]). The narrow definition used by authorities means that many other types of firms with direct or indirect state involvement are not included in official statistics, creating a potentially misleading impression of the state's involvement in the economy. For example, while the government reports that there are 257 directly owned joint-stock companies in Uzbekistan, a recent ADB study found that a further 329 JSCs were owned indirectly by the state, suggesting that almost three quarters of all such firms in the county were controlled, wholly or partially, by the state (Abdullaev, 2020[12]). Whilst it is encouraging to see the state recognise its control beyond the strict definition used by the authorities by including LLCs and JSCs in their calculations, there remain challenges in ensuring that analyses of state ownership are reflective of the *de facto* reality in the economy.

The government has already begun taking practical steps in implementing its privatisation agenda with technical assistance from IFIs, including the EBRD, the ADB, and the World Bank (World Bank, 2019[13]): tariffs have been raised to improve the economic viability of a number of utilities SOEs; legislation has been passed allowing the privatisation of non-agricultural land plots (Republic of Uzbekistan, 2019[14]); and, in 2019 a government resolution approved the selling of state shares in the chemical, hydrocarbon, mechanical engineering, banking and insurance sectors (Republic of Uzbekistan, 2019[15]). The government review of the vertically integrated national air company (NAK) is indicative of the its SOE reform intentions, with a presidential decree already reorganising the functions of NAK into new legal entities with a plan to engage in PPPs for the operation of the previous monopoly's assets (Republic of Uzbekistan, 2018[10]). The privatisation process must contend with what remains a fragmentary and unconsolidated legal landscape, which weighs on the administration and valuation of assets that may be privatised. For example, the law that determines the valuation of SOEs and state assets dates from 1992 and has never been amended, which may create difficulties in the accurate valuation of assets in the contemporary context.

5.2.5. *A clearer and more liberal regulatory framework is being put in place to support foreign investment*

In 2020, a new *Law on Investment and Investment Activities* (LoI) was enacted, replacing and expanding earlier laws from 1998 on foreign investment and investor protection, among others. An investment law can help provide transparency and clarity in a country's investment regime, stipulating the conditions for market access, as well as the protection of investment and the settlement of disputes. Many governments, particularly among OECD members, regulate investment through laws of more general application, but over 100 countries have enacted a specific investment law as a signalling device to potential investors.

Box 5.1. The 2020 *Law on Investment and Investment Activities of Uzbekistan*

The 2020 LoI is designed to systematise existing laws and by-laws and to level the playing field for foreign and domestic investors. As such, it applies to both foreign and domestic investors, although it excludes many forms of investment, such as those carried out under production sharing agreements, concession contracts and public-private partnerships, as well as in special economic zones. It is therefore unlikely to apply to many high-value natural resources and infrastructure investment projects, among others, where project-specific contractual arrangements with the state are commonplace. At the same time, it is unclear whether laws governing these other areas of activity (such as PPPs or SEZs, or project-specific contracts with the state) can supersede clauses in the LoI, thereby providing the government a loophole for expropriation or nationalisation. The question of legal hierarchy is one that the government must clarify for businesses, domestic and international alike, so that they can have certainty over the legal finality of acts such as the LoI. For investments falling within the scope of the LoI, the new law retains a broad set of generous protections, many of which apply equally to foreign and domestic investments. It includes a general principle of non-discrimination and guarantees of national treatment, protection from nationalisation (although not indirect expropriation) and transferability of funds abroad.

The new law also addresses an issue faced by investors in certain former Soviet republics, notably the attempts by some parts of central and regional governments to nullify licences for foreign investment projects under the pretext of violations of environmental or other regulations. It also insulates covered investors against detrimental regulatory changes by providing regulatory stability for a period of ten years from the time of the initial investment. While stabilisation guarantees are common in the region, they are far less common in other regions of the world as they can severely tie the hands of governments. An alternative – and more flexible – approach might be to include a provision on indirect expropriation in the law itself, subject to certain clear exceptions.

The new law introduces a four-stage process for resolving disputes concerning foreign investments. While there is some ambiguity in the drafting of the relevant provisions, the new law appears to list these four stages as mandatory and consecutive steps. An investor may only seek to commence international arbitration proceedings against the state if it has first attempted to resolve a dispute through negotiations, mediation and litigation in the Uzbek courts. The new law envisages the possibility of investor-state arbitration under investment treaties or contracts but stops short of providing open-ended consent of the state to arbitrate all investment disputes.

The OECD FDI Regulatory Restrictiveness Index demonstrates that Uzbekistan is relatively open to foreign investment. The country is in line with OECD average for statutory restrictions and outperforming other countries in the region included in the FDI Index, such as Kazakhstan, Kyrgyzstan and Mongolia (Figure 5.2)

Figure 5.2. OECD FDI Regulatory Restrictiveness Index: Uzbekistan (2020)

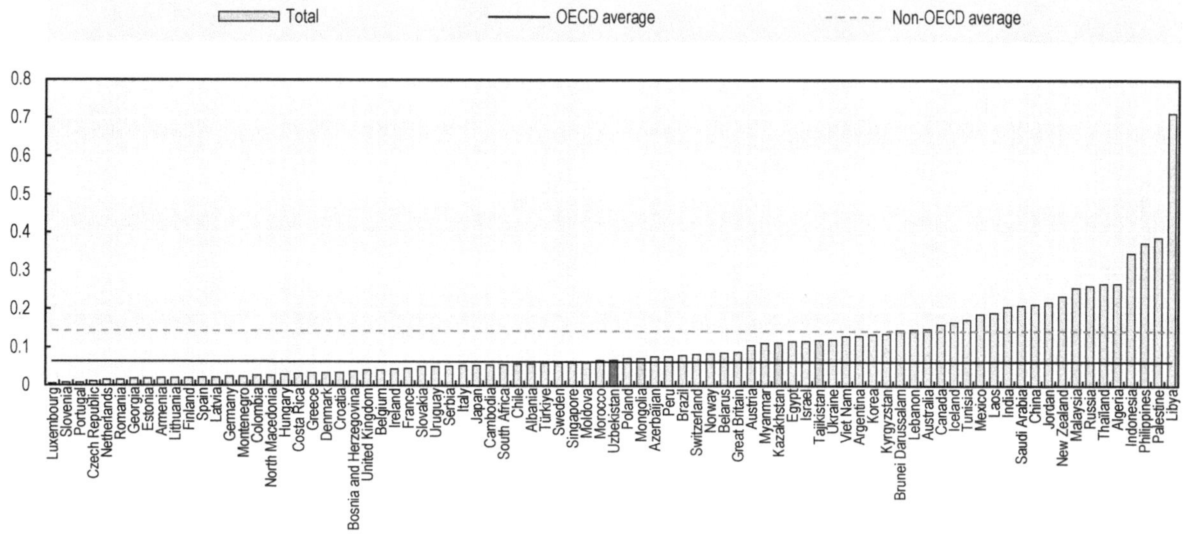

Note: 0 = open; 1 = closed.
Source: (OECD, 2023[16])

Restrictions remain for mass media, telecommunications, power generation, business services and other sectors and are particularly high in media, financial and business services (Figure 5.3). Some sectoral restrictions are fairly common, and reflect national concerns, but others could be re-evaluated to assess whether their intended impact justifies the possible deterrent effect they might have on inflows. This is particularly the case in the financial and business service sectors. Beyond the immediate impact on inflows, governments should also consider how restrictions affect downstream industries and consumers. At the very least, the government should communicate restrictions clearly on the online investment portal. As sectors currently dominated by SOEs are to be opened up, conditions for foreign investors' participation in the privatisation process will also need to be clearly defined and communicated. The EBRD is currently working with the government on a new law on privatisation, and is encouraging the government to ensure the law improves transparency surrounding the privatisation process and the participation of international investors therein.

Sectoral FDI incentives are numerous in the industrial, hospitality, pharmaceuticals and natural-resource sectors and mostly consist of tax benefits. Companies operating in Special Economic Zones (SEZ) also benefit from tax incentives, as well as customs benefits and services. There are currently twelve SEZs in the country, some of which have a sectoral focus (pharmaceuticals, sport, agriculture and tourism) (Dentons, 2019[6]). Whilst the laws for SEZs may be fairly clearly established, uncertainty arises concerning the interaction of national laws with these demarcated jurisdictions. This issue is not limited to Uzbekistan; across the region the issue of "legal hierarchy", i.e., understanding definitively how national legislation interacts with SEZ rules, creates uncertainty in the legal environment for business. Plans to reform these zones, better define their objectives and reassess incentive packages have been discussed but have not yet materialised according to the CCI.

Figure 5.3. OECD FDI Regulatory Restrictiveness Index: Sectoral restrictions in Uzbekistan (2020)

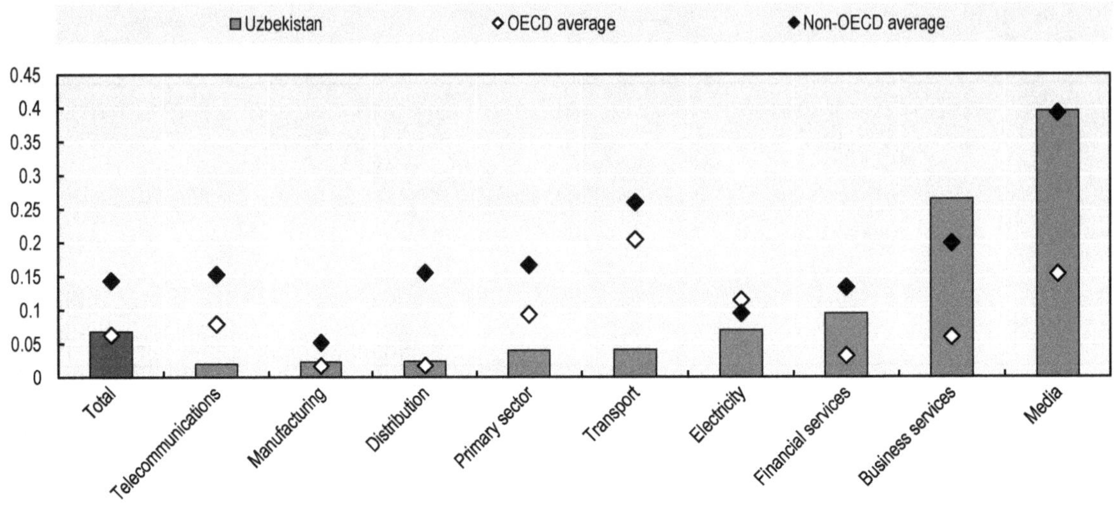

Note: 0 = open; 1 = closed.
Source: (OECD, 2023[16])

Limited progress has been made in liberalising key factor markets such as transport and land, but the purchase and transfer of the latter remain difficult. Foreign participation in the privatisation process of non-agricultural land is, however, possible only through local incorporation. Foreign investors and foreign-owned companies established in Uzbekistan are allowed to hold lease titles to land, but they are subject to different rules regarding the needed authorisation by the state in relation to leasing such lands. Foreign investors and foreign-owned companies require approval by the Cabinet of Ministers, while domestically-owned legal entities require approval only from district and cities *khokim* (governor). The dual process, and the existence of specific regulations on granting land plots to foreign legal and individuals (e.g. in Tashkent; see the "Decree of the Cabinet of Ministers on granting land plots to foreign legal and natural persons in Tashkent"), raise concerns about discriminatory treatment against foreign investors and are reflected in the OECD FDI Regulatory Restrictiveness Index.

As it continues to open up additional sectors of the economy to foreign investors, the government should prioritise ensuring that the LoI and related legislation are properly implemented. This should involve a concerted effort to raise the capacity of government agencies and to develop the capabilities of the MIIT to help with implementation and investor needs. In particular, Uzbekistan has recently created an Investment Promotion Agency under the MIIT that could be the entry point for investors and inform them of regulatory requirements and recent changes, as well as helping them meet these requirements (OECD, Forthcoming[17]). Stability of stakeholders is an essential feature of effective investment relations that is regularly cited by investors.

Effective Investment Promotion Agencies (IPAs) in OECD members, such as Turkey and Ireland, are active generators of investment and knowledge centres for investors, beyond promotion and image building activities (President of Turkey's Investment Office, 2019[18]). Uzbekistan's IPA could go beyond information provision and deliver advisory and aftercare services for investors, including on regulatory aspects by co-ordinating with other agencies, especially tax authorities and licensing bodies, to avoid multiplicity of contacts and inconsistent administrative procedures.

The government should also strive to remove further sectoral restrictions for investors, including in the financial and business service sectors. It could also communicate restrictions clearly on the online investment portal. As sectors currently dominated by SOEs are to be opened up, conditions for foreign investors' participation in the privatisation process will need to be clearly defined and communicated.

5.3. Complimentary pro-competition reforms are necessary to address *de facto* barriers to investment

As noted in the introduction to this chapter, respondents highlighted competition policies as the weakest aspect of the legal framework for business in Uzbekistan, as well as being the area where respondents had seen the least progress over the past five years. When asked to give their opinion on three specific aspects of competition policy – control of market dominance and monopoly practices, measures in place against cartels and concerted practices, and concentration control – progress was rated as weak by over 50% in each instance (as high as 67% for market dominance and monopoly practices). The government of Uzbekistan is aware of the need to seriously improve competition policies if the broader ambition of private sector development and investment attraction is to be achieved, and in 2022 solicited OECD help in this area (OECD, 2022[2]).

The picture that emerges is one where the private sector continues to be beset by a myriad of competition-related issues (for example, the practice of preferential lending to SOEs below market rates, tax breaks for certain SOEs and even quotas in certain industries), hampering incentives to invest and grow. Yet as with the general legal and regulatory framework for business outlined in section 5.2, these complaints and concerns come amidst a large number of changes that have been put in place precisely to level the playing field for private business. That firms have yet to feel the benefits of these legal reforms speaks to challenges with implementation, the scope of the legal reforms made so far, and a complicated range of adjacent reforms (such as in land and other factor markets, or corporatisation and privatisation of state assets) that that are required to level playing the field between public and private enterprise.

5.3.1. Reforms to competition law and enforcement have been a key part of the broader reform process

Competition law and policy have formed an important part of the ongoing, broader reform agenda of the government of Uzbekistan. One of the first important steps towards creating a strong competition framework was the establishment of the Competition Promotion and Consumer Protection Committee of the Republic of Uzbekistan (ACRU) in 2019, which was achieved by institutionally reorganising a larger regulator that had previously overseen both competition and privatisation policy. The ACRU, which is designed to be an independent regulatory, has the task of overseeing the implementation of competition and other market-related policies, such as consumer protection, advertising, and tackling corruption that distorts competition.

The regulator is already very active. Since its inception, it has already assessed more than 5,500 legislative acts in terms of their possible impact on market competition, conducted more than 2,000 antitrust investigations, cleared around 500 mergers, and has organised around 100 advocacy events aimed at improving the awareness of public bodies regarding the importance of market competition (OECD, 2022[2]).

In addition to the institutional changes to support competition policy, the government drafted a new law on competition in 2022. The law codified a number of important changes to the country's competition framework, including: new rules for vertical agreements; an extended list of behaviours considered abuse of dominance; merger control in cases of establishment of joint ventures; enhanced enforcement powers, including the right to issue fines; the inclusion of state aid regulation with ACRU responsible for oversight; regulation on the extent of the state in the economy; and a framework for regulating digital markets.

Following the assessment conducted by the OECD in 2022, the Organisation made a number of targeted recommendations, which, if implemented, would directly address many of the concerns that firms continue to report. These recommendations included improving the independence and mandate of the ACRU, including by ensuring that the ACRU has the budget and resources it needs to fulfil its mandate, improving both the legal provisions for addressing cartels and abuses of dominance as well as ensuring adequate powers for enforcement, and ensuring effective powers and procedures for the ACRU to be able to promote competitive neutrality.

Table 5.1. An Introduction to Competition Law and Policy in Uzbekistan: overview of recommendations

Recommendation	Competition policy
1	Clarify the focus and goals of the competition policy
	Institutional design and framework conditions
2	Ensure that the appointment of ACRU's Chairperson is based on objective, transparent and qualitative criteria, including the experience and expertise of the candidate, and determine an exhaustive list of grounds for the early dismissal from office
3	Ensure that ACRU's institutional set-up allows for (i) sufficient separation between competition and non-competition related mandates, and (ii) sufficient staff to execute the competition (and non-competition) related tasks
4	Ensure a sufficient and securely funded budget for ACRU to execute its mandate effectively and independently
5	Increase ACRU's operational independence to allow for more effective enforcement
6	Increase the judiciary's and courts' knowledge of, and familiarity with, economic concepts and principles in the application of competition enforcement decisions
7	Engage more actively in international co-operation
	Legal framework and enforcement
8	Improve substantive provisions on cartels and abuse of dominance
9	Ensure adequate powers for effective antitrust enforcement
10	Clarify the substantive merger test; extend assessment time limits
11	Increase transparency of ACRU's enforcement decisions and principles
12	Ensure effective powers and procedures for ACRU to promote competitive neutrality
	Continued improvement
13	Ensure continuous optimisation of the enforcement framework through international benchmarking

Source: (OECD, 2022[2])

These recent changes to Uzbekistan's competition law, on top of the conditions that were already in place, mean that the country has a strong *de jure* competition law regime, with Uzbekistan performing well against its regional peers in an international benchmarking exercise conducted by the OECD (OECD, 2022[2]). Its highest scores were in the categories of enforcement policies against anti-competitive behaviour and advocacy, and lowest in the area of probity of investigation. There nevertheless remains a significant deal of work to be done to improve the legal framework for competition, though the government's decision to submit to an OECD review of competition policy is in itself an important indication of the seriousness with which the government takes the matter.

References

Abdullaev, U. (2020), *State-Owned Enterprises in Uzbekistan: Taking Stock and Some Reform Priorities*, ADBI Working Papers, No. ADBI Working Paper 1068, https://www.adb.org/sites/default/files/publication/560601/adbi-wp1068.pdf. [12]

Dentons (2019), *Doing business in Uzbekistan.* [6]

European Union (2019), *European Union Supports Uzbekistan's Accession to WTO*, https://eeas.europa.eu/delegations/burkina-faso/59579/european-union-supports-uzbekistan%E2%80%99s-accession-world-trade-organization-wto_en. [27]

ITF (2019), *Enhancing Connectivity and Freight in Central Asia*, OECD Publishing, Paris, https://www.itf-oecd.org/sites/default/files/docs/connectivity-freight-central-asia_2.pdf. [25]

OECD (2023), *FDI Regulatory Restrictiveness Index*, OECD Publishing, Paris, https://stats.oecd.org/Index.aspx?DataSetCode=FDIINDEX. [32]

OECD (2023), *OECD FDI Regulatory Restrictiveness Index*, Uzbekistan, OECD Publishing, Paris, https://stats.oecd.org/Index.aspx?DataSetCode=FDIINDEX. [16]

OECD (2023), *OECD Trade Facilitation Indicators*, Uzbekistan, OECD Publishing, Paris, https://www.oecd.org/trade/topics/trade-facilitation/. [31]

OECD (2022), *An Introduction to Competition Law and Policy in Uzbeksitan*, OECD Publishing, Paris, https://www.oecd.org/daf/competition/an-introduction-to-competition-law-and-policy-in-uzbekistan.pdf. [2]

OECD (2021), *Beyond COVID-19: Prospects for Economic Recovery in Central Asia*, OECD Publishing, Paris, https://www.oecd.org/eurasia/Beyond_COVID%2019_Central%20Asia.pdf. [20]

OECD (2021), *Boosting the Internationalisation of Firms through better Export Promotion Policies in Uzbekistan*, OECD Eurasia Policy Insights, OECD Publishing, Paris, https://www.oecd.org/eurasia/Monitoring_Review_Uzbekistan_ENG.pdf. [23]

OECD (2021), *Improving the Legal Environment for Business and Investment in Central Asia*, OECD Publishing, Paris, https://www.oecd.org/eurasia/Improving-LEB-CA-ENG%2020%20April.pdf. [1]

OECD (2020), *COVID-19 Crisis Response in Central Asia*, OECD Publishing, Paris, https://read.oecd-ilibrary.org/view/?ref=129_129634-ujyjsqu30i&title=COVID-19-crisis-response-in-central-asia. [19]

OECD (2017), *Boosting SME Internationalisation in Uzbekistan through better Export Promotion Policies*, OECD Publishing, Paris, https://www.oecd.org/eurasia/competitiveness-programme/central-asia/Uzbekistan_Peer_review_note_dec2017_final.pdf. [24]

OECD (Forthcoming), *Investment promotion practices in Eurasia*. [17]

OECD (Forthcoming), *Monitoring Report: Improving the Legal Environment for Business and Investment in Central Asia*, OECD Publishing, Paris. [33]

President of Turkey's Investment Office (2019), *Official website*, http://www.invest.gov.tr. [18]

Republic of Uzbekistan (2022), *Development Strategy of New Uzbekistan for 2022-2026*, https://uzembassy.kz/upload/userfiles/files/Development%20Strategy%20of%20Uzbekistan.pdf. [22]

Republic of Uzbekistan (2019), *Draft Tax Code*, https://regulation.gov.uz/ru/document/7232-nalogovy_kodeks_respubliki_uzbekistan (accessed on 2020). [9]

Republic of Uzbekistan (2019), *Law No. ZRU-522 "On privatization of non-agricultural land plots"*. [15]

Republic of Uzbekistan (2019), *On Further Measures for the Implementation of the Mechanisms for Attracting FDI into the Economy No. 4300*. [14]

Republic of Uzbekistan (2019), *Reform Roadmap 2019-21*. [4]

Republic of Uzbekistan (2018), *Decree of the President of the Republic of Uzbekistan on Measures to Further Reduce and Simplify Licensing and Licensing Procedures in the Field of Entrepreneurial Activity, as well as Improving Business Conditions*, http://www.lex.uz/ru/docs/3676962 (accessed on 13 May 2019). [7]

Republic of Uzbekistan (2018), *Presidential Decree 5584 On Measures to Improve Civil Aviation*. [10]

Republic of Uzbekistan (2017), *National Development Strategy 2017-21*. [3]

Republic of Uzbekistan (2017), *State Programme for the Realisation of the Strategy on Five Priority Areas for Development of the Republic of Uzbekistan 2017-2021*. [30]

Republic of Uzbekistan (2006), *Law on State Owned Enteprises*, https://nrm.uz/contentf?doc=372435_polojenie_o_gosudarstvennyh_predpriyatiyah_(prilojenie_n_1_k_postanovleniyu_km_ruz_ot_16_10_2006_g_n_215)&products=1_vse_zakonodatelstvo_uzbekistana. [11]

State Asset Management Agency of Uzbekistan (2020), *Privatization as a Driver of Economic Reform*. [28]

The State Committee of the Republic of Uzbekistan on Statistics (2023), *Small Business and Entrepreneurship*, The State Committee of the Republic of Uzbekistan on Statistics, Tashkent, https://stat.uz/en/official-statistics/small-business-and-entrepreneurship. [21]

World Bank (2022), *Uzbekistan: The Second Systematic Country Diagnostic*, World Bank, DC, https://documents1.worldbank.org/curated/en/933471650320792872/pdf/Toward-a-Prosperous-and-Inclusive-Future-The-Second-Systematic-Country-Diagnostic-for-Uzbekistan.pdf. [29]

World Bank (2021), *Assessing Uzbekistan's Transition: Country Economic Memorandum*, World Bank, DC, https://documents1.worldbank.org/curated/en/862261637233938240/pdf/Full-Report.pdf. [8]

World Bank (2020), *Doing Business 2020*, https://doi.org/10.1596/978-1-4648-1440-2. [26]

World Bank (2019), *Doing Business 2019: Uzbekistan, Training for Reform*, World Bank Group, DC, https://www.doingbusiness.org/content/dam/doingBusiness/country/u/uzbekistan/UZB.pdf. [5]

World Bank (2019), *Press Release: Support to Public Financial Management and State-Owned Enterprises Reforms to Benefit Uzbekistan's Citizens and Economy*. [13]

6 Skills and infrastructure for private sector digitalisation

While survey respondents were positive about digital opportunities in the country, many expressed concerns regarding infrastructure and skills. The process of digitalisation will profoundly shape Uzbekistan's economy and society in the years to come, just as it is doing across the OECD. Ensuring access to high-quality connectivity infrastructure and raising the level of digital skills in the workforce are essential for enabling the private sector to make the most of the opportunities of digitalisation.

6.1. Survey observations and overview

The digital transformation is having a profound impact on Uzbekistan's private sector. Many of the consequences of digitalisation are well-known, shared, and analysed, and the OECD continues to do extensive work on how best to take advantage of the opportunities of digitalisation whilst mitigating the socio-economic risks the digital transition can pose. Digitalisation can offer new opportunities for firm organisation and production, as well as how crucial government services are administered, while the ever-increasing value of data as an economic input is pushing the frontiers of innovation in both public and private sectors. At the same time, as the contribution of digital technologies and services continues to increase its share of value added in both manufacturing and services, who has the skills and capacities to take advantage of digitalisation will have significant implications for the inclusivity of economic growth.

Enabling the private sector – and society more broadly – to make the most of the opportunities offered by the digital transformation requires a range of different policy interventions. For one, firms can only digitise their activities – for example, through the adoption of IT solutions, be they simple or advanced, to improve productivity – if the basic digital and connectivity infrastructure is in place. This means having access to high-quality internet, fixed and cellular; access to ICT equipment and software; and the availability of more complex forms of digital infrastructure, such as cloud computing. It also means having access to the skills and knowledge necessary to apply digital technologies and to derive new insights and innovations from them. Finally, it means having access to the capital necessary to invest in the above, and a regulatory environment that fosters digitalisation rather than constraints it.

As in all economies, the challenges facing policymakers in fostering the digital transformation involve a combination of internationally shared barriers mapped onto local conditions. In Uzbekistan, this is particularly true for challenges around digital skills, access to finance, and competition in key network sectors. The government has declared its ambition to drive the digital transformation of the country's economy, with its strategic objectives codified in the Digital Uzbekistan 2030 project, which places a particular focus on the digitalisation of the public administration, education, healthcare and agriculture (Box 6.1).

These localised challenges were identified by respondents to the BCA survey, many of whom underscored their enthusiasm for digital opportunities in Uzbekistan but also their frustration at how underdeveloped framework conditions prevented them from making the most of these opportunities. Respondents to the survey reported a high level of optimism for the opportunities presented by digitalisation, as well as generally high level of digitalisation within their firms. Some 80% of respondents considered digitalisation to present opportunities for their business activities in Uzbekistan (37% significant opportunities, 43% some opportunities).

Box 6.1. Digital Uzbekistan 2030

Digital Uzbekistan-2030 aims to actively develop Uzbekistan's digital economy. Special attention is given to public administration, education, healthcare and agriculture. The road map for the implementation of the *Digital Uzbekistan 2030* strategy for 2020-2022 incorporates these dimensions, with individual actions, objectives, and targets set out for each of them. From 2023, the NDS will be implemented on the basis of two-year programs approved by the Cabinet of Ministers.

These programs are based on the results achieved, target indicators, and the development of digital technologies for each preceding and upcoming period. The dimensions to develop during the 2020-2022 period with example initiatives are the:

- development of **electronic government**:
  - E-ID cards for employees of state bodies
  - An open data portal for procurement, registration, and statistics
  - E-payment systems for all mandatory payments
- development of **digital industry**:
  - Technopark residency status and benefits for firms in IT training, software, hardware, robotics, Internet export services, data storage, data processing…
  - Digital transformation of commercial banks
- development of **digital education**:
  - Compensate up to 50% of the cost of obtaining international IT certificates in high-demand areas for individuals
  - Open digital training centres in each district and city
  - Gradually open more than 200 specialised schools providing training in computer science and IT subjects
- development of **digital infrastructure**:
  - Connect every settlement to the Internet with a data transfer speed of at least 10 Mbit/s
  - Provide high-speed Internet access to all popular tourist destinations

As of Q1 2023, the implementation of over half of the 400 priority projects has begun.

All respondents to the BCA reported that at least 50% of their business operations had been digitised, while 41% of respondents reported that around 75% of operations were digitised. Whilst the sample is small, these figures nevertheless suggest a relatively high level of digital penetration in the European business community in Uzbekistan, though it would be necessary to compare with the domestic business community with a larger sample size to determine whether such levels were representative throughout the country.

It was notable that a significant majority of respondents reported that they used advanced tools. This included 79% of respondents who used customer relationship manager software (CRM) or some form of data analytics, which suggests a relatively high level of digital maturity of European firms operating in Uzbekistan. The rate of firms using cloud-based data solutions (52%) and digital communications (54%) further underscores the notable digitalisation of the surveyed firms.

However, as with the green transition, the key barrier to the further adoption and use of digital technologies by the surveyed firms appears to be primarily infrastructure related. An overwhelming majority (83%) of respondents underscored the importance of improving internet speed and quality for digitalisation, whilst another 43% emphasised the need to improve data security infrastructure. Other issues related to the need to develop online payment systems (33%), improve the digital skills and qualifications of the labour force (30%), and to improve the quality of the regulatory framework for online commerce (30%).

The purpose of this short chapter is to expand upon two areas identified in the BCA survey as problematic for the digitalisation of the private sector in Uzbekistan. The first concerns the digital and connectivity infrastructure available to firms. The OECD Going Digital Toolkit gives a framework for assessing the degree of digital transformation in both member and non-member economies, and this section combines some of the commonly used indicators of digitalisation with other data, such as investment in digital and intangible capital, to give an overview of the extent of digitalisation in Uzbekistan. The second section picks up another key barrier for private sector digitalisation – skills. This section draws on work conducted by the OECD Eurasia Competitiveness Programme on digital skills in Uzbekistan and presents some of the key findings from this work.

6.2. Infrastructure and connectivity gaps must be bridged to advance private sector digitalisation

The rate and depth of digitalisation in Uzbekistan, as in any country, is shaped by a number of important infrastructure-related framework conditions and the diffusion of digital technologies. It is precisely the lack of development of these framework conditions that BCA respondents identified as the major barrier to digitalisation in Uzbekistan. The OECD collects a wide range of data on issues such as broadband diffusion and access, data consumption, enterprise usage and geographical coverage, but non-member countries are not yet included in these statistics, making it difficult to conduct accurate international benchmarking. Nevertheless, using a range of OECD indicators, including the OECD Broadband Portal indicators, this section presents a brief assessment of the development of the supportive infrastructure necessary for digitalisation of Uzbekistan's private sector.

The cost of fixed broadband in Uzbekistan is relatively high, at 2.1% GNI, slightly above the SDG target of 2%, though significantly lower than in some Central Asian economies, such as Tajikistan, Turkmenistan and Kyrgyzstan (Figure 6.1). The cost of access to the Internet in Uzbekistan is nevertheless converging with the OECD and trending towards to the SDG target. This is a positive sign, one that indicates a relatively low-cost barrier to Internet access, and which in theory should make digital opportunities accessible to a large number of households and firms.

Figure 6.1. Cost of fixed broadband access as percentage of GNI (2021)

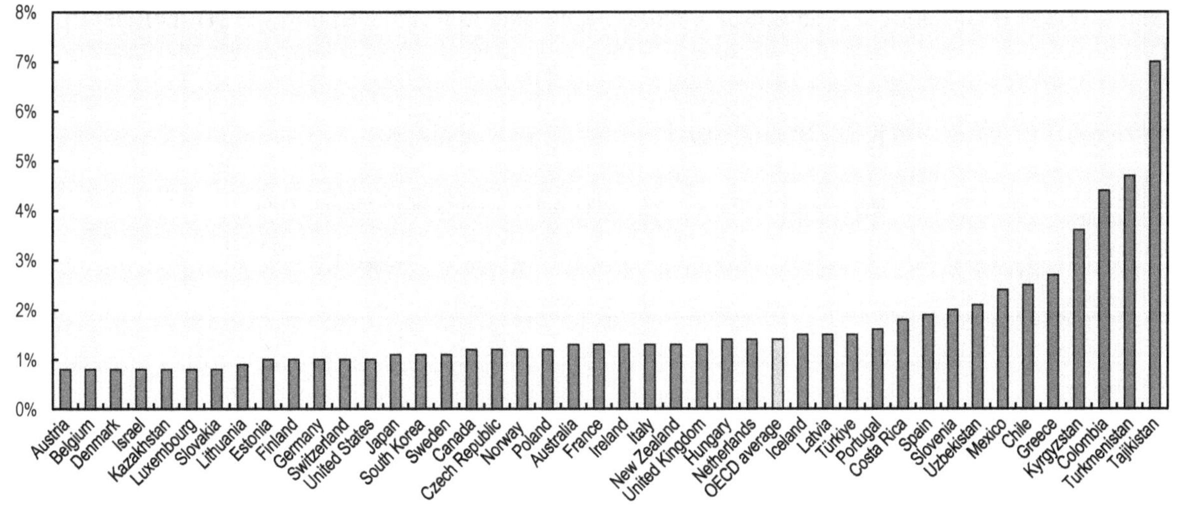

Source: (ITU, 2023[1])

Yet whilst the cost of Internet access is relatively low at the national level, the quality of connectivity infrastructure is highly variable across Uzbekistan's regions. For example, the total length of fibre-optic communication lines at the regional level seems to be more strongly correlated with gross regional output than with population size or density (Figure 6.2).The implication is that the extent of the development of the connectivity infrastructure necessary for the digital transformation is greater in areas of higher economic output, regardless of whether these are more or less populated (Figure 6.2)

Figure 6.2. Regional connectivity infrastructure and economic development (2021)

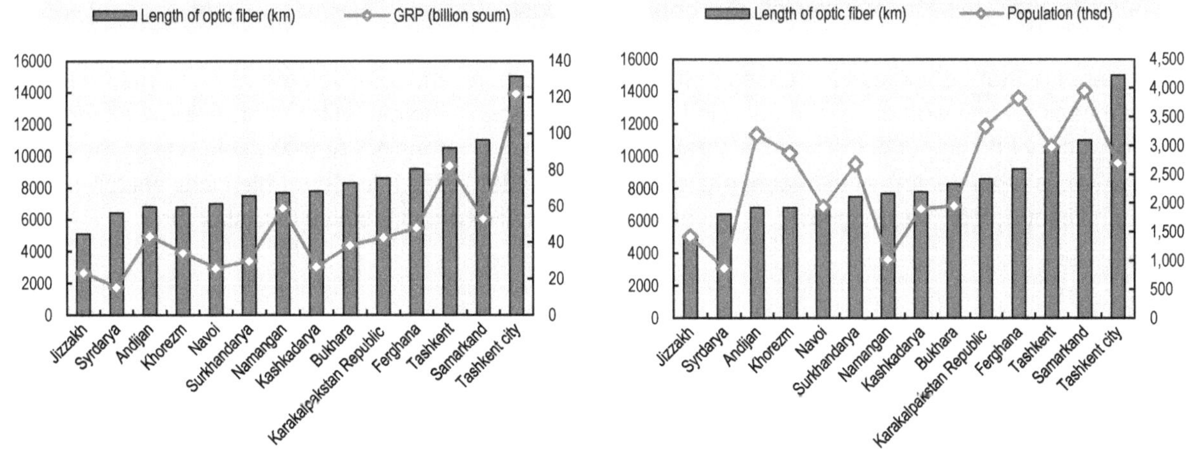

Note: OECD calculations

Source: (The State Committee of the Republic of Uzbekistan on Statistics, 2023[2]), (The State Committee of the Republic of Uzbekistan on Statistics, 2023[3])

One clear trend in Uzbekistan that has significant implications for the digital transition is underinvestment in ICTs. Investment in ICTs in Uzbekistan amounted to only 1.65% of total GFCF, significantly below the OECD average of 11.4%, and further still behind the leading OECD member Sweden (20%) and the Czech Republic (17%) (Figure 6.3). Relative to the size of the economy, the level is similarly low (equivalent to 0.65% GDP), comparable only to Poland among OECD members (0.78% GDP).

Figure 6.3. Investment in ICTs: Uzbekistan in international context

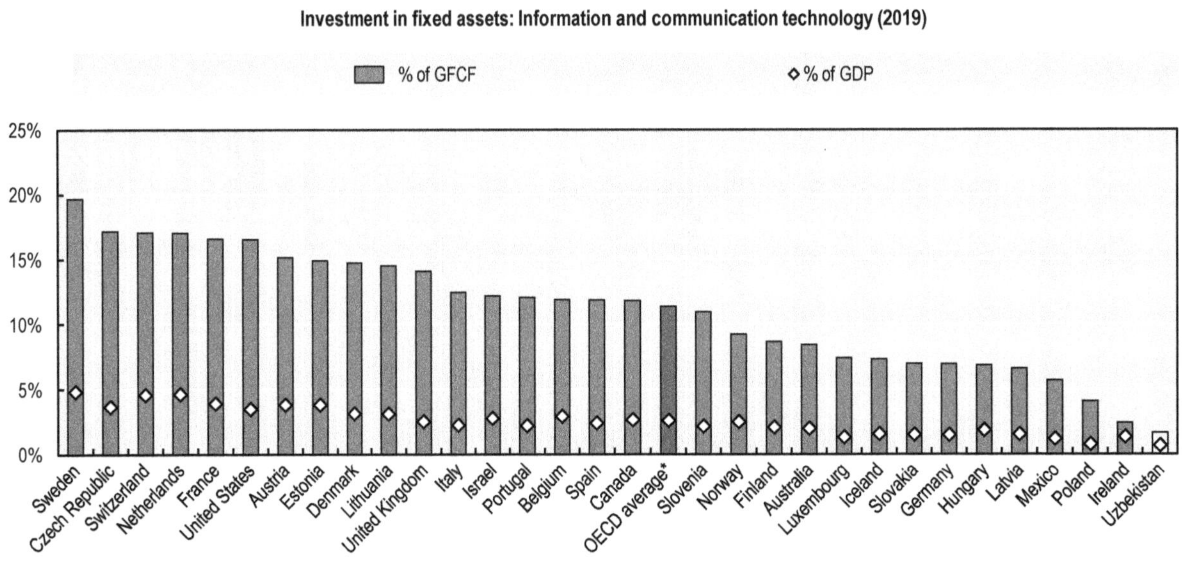

Note: *The OECD average does not include Chile, Colombia, Costa Rica, Greece, Japan, Korea, New Zealand.
Source: (OECD, 2023[4])

There are factors that may account for the relatively low level of investment in ICTs and digital technologies in Uzbekistan. For example, since the government began to liberalise foreign trade, there has been a significant rise in imports of capital goods, largely driven by public investment, in part due to the need to modernise and replenish the country's industrial base. This may in part account for the relatively low share of investment in ICTs (and indeed other forms of intangible capital). At the same time, it is imperative that Uzbekistan increases both the relative share and total volume of investment in these assets if its firms and workers are to be able to take advantage of the digital transformation, ensuring that the productivity and output of the country's nascent private sector does not further diverge from the OECD average. As in other sectors of the economy, competition issues in the telecommunications sector may act as a significant barrier to raising levels of investment in digital and connectivity infrastructure.

6.3. Firms need new skills to succeed in the digital transition

Firms need new skills and capacities to succeed in the digital transition. The ability of private sector firms to make the most of the opportunities presented by the digitalisation transition, and to ensure that they are not left behind by competitors both domestically and internationally, depends on the capacities of firms to use a range of digital technologies, as well as complementary capacities in other areas necessary to identify commercial or organisational use cases for those same technologies too (such as management skills that reflect how digitalisation can affect firm organisation).

The ability of a manufacturing SME in Uzbekistan to innovate in how they organise themselves or how they produce depends on their ability to derive new data and insights from those data using digital tools. It is for this reason that, in a study on the impact of various policy interventions and framework conditions on the diffusion of digital technologies in the EU, the OECD found that the intervention with the greatest single impact was upgrading technical and managerial skills of firms(Figure 6.4). At the same time, firms must have the internal capacities and knowledge to recognise the *value* in using digital tools for their business, and to have the skills necessary to recognise opportunities where digitalisation would be of use to them.

Figure 6.4. Impact of selected policy interventions on improving productivity

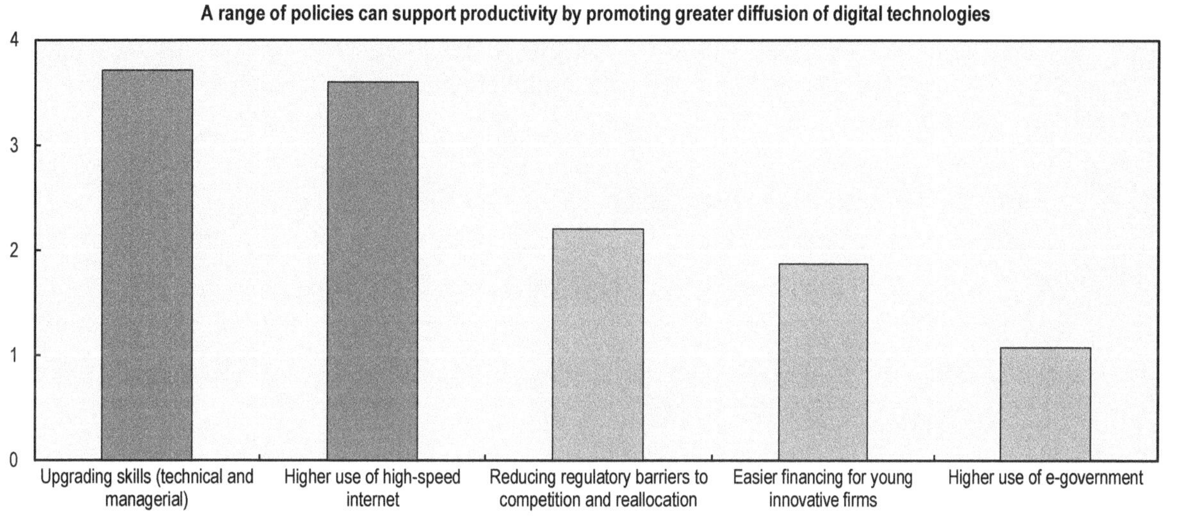

Note: Effect on multifactor productivity of the average EU firm of closing half of the gap with best-performing EU countries in a range of structural and policy areas, after 3 years
Source: (OECD, 2019[5])

The type of skills that the workforce needs to make the most of the digital transition are manifold. In certain cases, new types of jobs and the changing nature of existing ones require job holders to have a mix of technical and high-level cognitive skills, for example, database management skills and related data analytical skills. In some professions, proficiency in coding languages such as Python and Java, or knowledge of and experience with machine learning, data science and visualisation techniques in others. These are advanced skills, ones which are not widely held even in OECD countries (1% of the population), but they are nevertheless important for Uzbekistan and other transition economies if they are not to be left behind by new forms of value creation, drivers of productivity, and innovation (OECD, 2022[6]). At the same time, more 'basic' skills, such as a familiarity with widely used software or experience with social media platforms are increasingly important to a wide range of industries, beyond the traditional confines of the

'ICT' sector. Whilst there are of course sector- and industry-specific digital skills needs, the whole-of-economy significance of digitalisation requires an inclusive approach to digital skills development.

While it is clear that digitalisation offers significant opportunities for innovation and productivity growth for Uzbekistan's SMEs, the uneven diffusion of infrastructure and skills risks aggravating productivity gaps between firms due to difficulties in financing digital technologies and the related intangible capital necessary to use them effectively. Access to finance challenges are long-standing barriers to firm growth in Uzbekistan, but the banking sector's stringent collateral requirements are particularly difficult for SMEs in the digital context, where much of the investment is in intangible capital (skills, software and other forms of intellectual property). Ensuring broad access to the skills and capacities necessary to make the most of digitalisation is therefore also important for inclusion, be it at the industrial level (i.e., between firms and industries with more or less investment capacity), regional level (i.e., between SMEs in Tashkent and major industrial hubs and more rural areas of the country), or socio-economic level (i.e., gendered differences in terms of access to digital skills).

The level of digital skills in Uzbekistan is significantly behind the OECD average, as well as trailing the level observed in neighbouring Kazakhstan (Figure 6.5). Worryingly, this is true across the basic, standard, and advanced skills categories, suggesting that the labour force in Uzbekistan remains underequipped to use even the more basic of digital technologies and to recognise potential applications for them in their own businesses, or indeed in the context of a start-up or innovation. Raising the general level of digital skills should be a priority for the government in its pursuit of private sector competitiveness. Efforts should be made to begin digital skills training early in the education system, ensuring that new labour market entrants are equipped with the skills they need to succeed, as well as mitigating the development of skills-related bottlenecks in the labour market as digital technologies continue to change how firms work and produce.

Figure 6.5. Overview of digital skills: Uzbekistan, Kazakhstan and OECD average

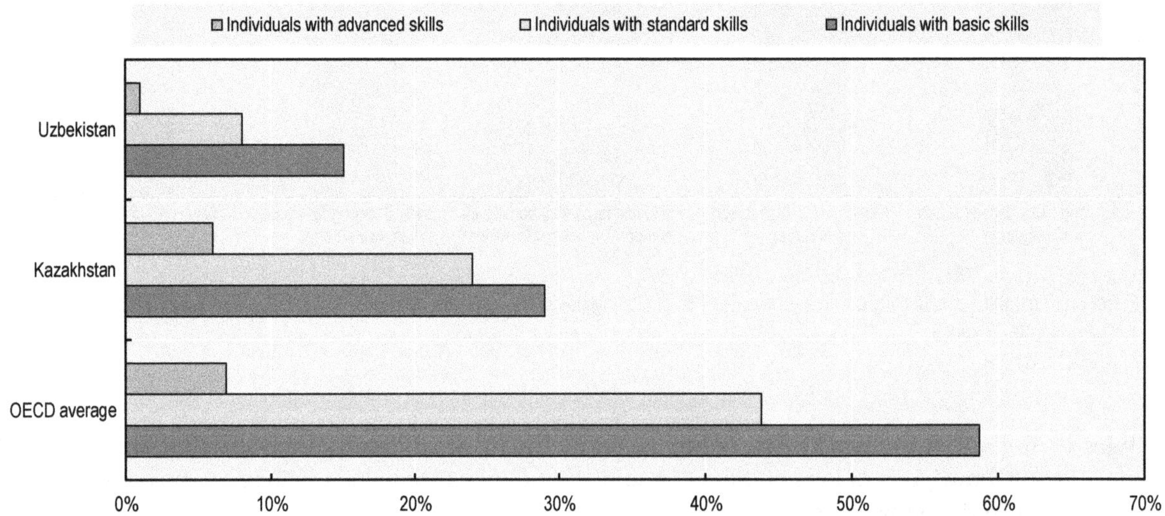

Note: As a percentage of the population. *Data was not available for Australia, Canada, Costa Rica, Israel, New Zealand, United States. Data for Uzbekistan is from 2018-2020, data for Kazakhstan is from 2019-2020. Observations for OECD countries go from 2013 to 2020.
Source: (ITU, 2023[1])

The difference in digital skills levels in Uzbekistan and peer countries is particularly stark in the areas which one might associate as productivity-enhancing. where the person uses their digital knowledge to create new knowledge and insights from data, or to innovate and improve

communications (WEF, 2020[7]) (OECD, 2021[8]). For example, Uzbekistan significantly lags Kazakhstan, which is close to the OECD average, in using an arithmetic formula in a spreadsheet, creating an electronic presentation, connecting new electronic devices, or downloading and configuring software (Figure 6.6) In part, this may also reflect the slow structural transformation of Uzbekistan, with many more people working in sectors and industries where the use of digital tools is generally lower (such as agriculture), but it nevertheless highlights the potential for significant skills-related labour shortages and bottlenecks as the economy continues to move towards higher-value adding activities where the advantages and effects of digitalisation are more obvious and prevalent. Greater data availability on digital skills and digital diffusion in the business community, for example in terms of firm size and industry, would allow for more targeted policy interventions should they be necessary.

Figure 6.6. Breakdown of digital skills: Uzbekistan, Kazakhstan and the OECD average (2019)

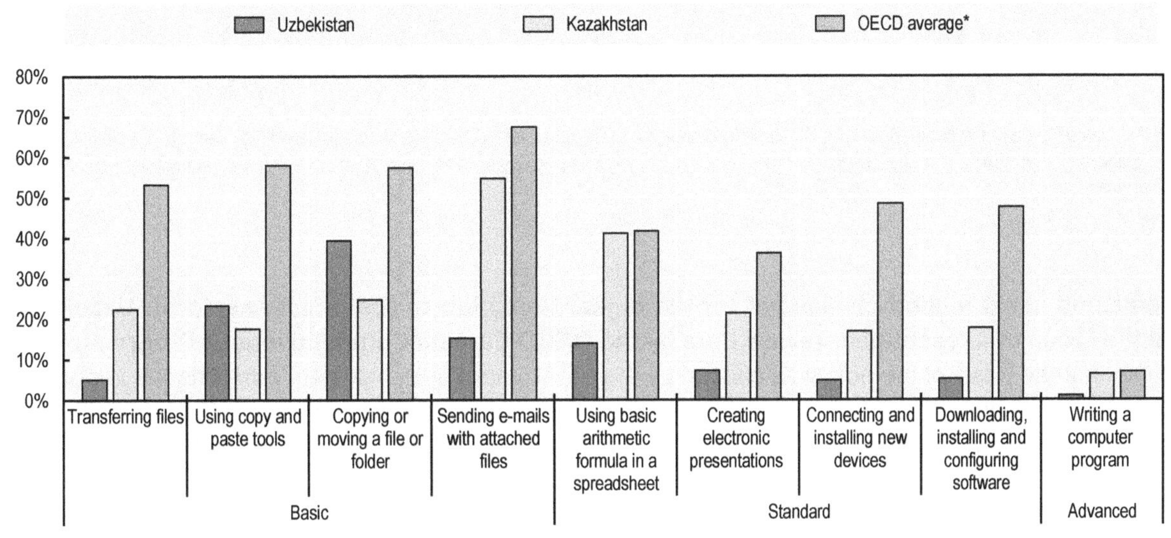

Note: As a percentage of the population. *Data was not available for Australia, Canada, Costa Rica, Israel, New Zealand, United States. Data for Uzbekistan is from 2018-2020, data for Kazakhstan is from 2019-2020. Observations for OECD countries go from 2013 to 2020.
Source: (ITU, 2023[1])

One characteristic of the digital skills landscape in Uzbekistan, as in Kazakhstan, is that the digital skills gap appears to be relatively ungendered. The gap between men and women in basic, standard and advanced skills significantly higher in the OECD than it is in Uzbekistan and Kazakhstan (Figure 6.7.)Given the generally low level of digital skills in Uzbekistan, the relatively narrow gender gap may be more representative of the broader availability of these skills rather than a positive trend in their development, with interviews for a 2023 peer review of digital skills in Uzbekistan noting that access to digital skills development is more limited for women. It is important to note that a country's historically important industries can create path dependencies in skills availability and development that can either enable or inhibit the private sector's digital – and green – transition (OECD, 2022[9]). If, for example, in a certain economy there has been a historically high importance of a given sector or industry where gender gaps are present, then it may follow that the starting point from which to develop digital skills may be uneven (e.g., if an industry in which digitalisation has clear potential to increase productivity and innovation, such as manufacturing, has had a historically significant gender gap in terms of employment or productivity, then there may be structural barriers to overcome to ensure that the development of digital skills is truly inclusive).

Figure 6.7. Gender differences in the digital skills gap: Uzbekistan, Kazakhstan and the OECD average (2019, in percentage points)

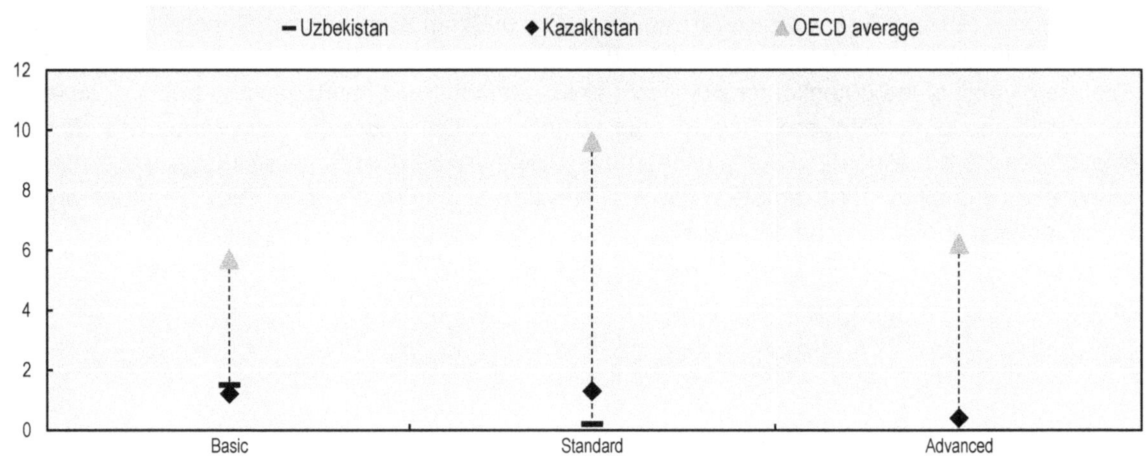

Note: As a percentage of the population. OECD estimations based on ITU data. Data was not available for Australia, Canada, Costa Rica, Israel, New Zealand, United States. Data for Uzbekistan is from 2018-2020, data for Kazakhstan is from 2019-2020. Observations for OECD countries go from 2013 to 2020.
Source: (ITU, 2023[1])

Addressing skills related challenges for the digital transition of the private sector in Uzbekistan was the focus of a recent peer review note by the OECD Eurasia Competitiveness Programme. It is notable that the focus of the note was chosen by the government of Uzbekistan, reflecting the importance placed by the authorities on the issue of digital skills in the country. The request also reflects a challenging reality in the country, that for all the enthusiasm expressed for digital opportunities through the BCA survey, uptake of digital technologies remains low (Portulans Institute, 2020[10]).

Smaller firms in Uzbekistan tend to be less aware of the digital skills support programmes available to them on a limited or zero cost basis. Governments generally play a coordinating role in managing the different actors and institutions involved in the digital transition, and part of that includes ensuring that the target of specific policies, in this case firms, are aware of the opportunities available to them. In Uzbekistan, despite there being a strong political commitment to supporting private sector digitalisation, as codified through the government's National Digital Strategy, there is a lack of clear policies to support digital upskilling in the private sector as well as a lack of awareness raising and outreach concerning those policies that do exist.

There is a general lack of awareness among Uzbekistan's private sector concerning the opportunities in the digital transition. This is particularly true for the country's smaller firms, which are often unaware both of the opportunities presented by digitalisation as well as the skills necessary to make the most of such opportunities. This is a particular challenge for Uzbekistan, whose geographical connectivity penalty means that it is imperative that domestic firms close the productivity gap with international firms if they are to be competitive abroad, something that is a long-standing policy objective of the government.

References

ITU (2023), *ITU Digital Development Dashboard*, ITU, World Telecommunication/ICT Indicators Database, https://www.itu.int/en/ITU-D/Statistics/Dashboards/Pages/Digital-Development.aspx. [1]

OECD (2023), *Digital Skills for Private Sector Competitiveness*, OECD Publishing, Paris. [16]

OECD (2023), *Invesment by asset*, OECD Publishing, Paris, https://data.oecd.org/gdp/investment-by-asset.htm. [4]

OECD (2022), *Going Digital to Advance Data Governance for Growth and Well-being*, OECD Publishing, https://www.oecd-ilibrary.org/docserver/e3d783b0-en.pdf?expires=1676886088&id=id&accname=ocid84004878&checksum=09D05160C9B561082FD490BBDA17AC86. [12]

OECD (2022), *OECD Reviews of Innovation Policy: Germany 2022: Building Agility for Successful Transitions*, OECD Reviews of Innovation Policy, OECD Publishing, Paris, https://doi.org/10.1787/50b32331-en. [9]

OECD (2022), *Skills for the Digital Transition: Assessing Recent Trends using Big Data*, OECD Publishing, Paris, https://www.oecd-ilibrary.org/docserver/38c36777-en.pdf?expires=1676976769&id=id&accname=ocid84004878&checksum=5BF20BE13D076B519F8C025F7ADC90E8. [6]

OECD (2021), *Emerging Trends in Communication Market Competition*, OECD Digital Economy Papers, No. No. 316, OECD Publishing, https://www.oecd-ilibrary.org/docserver/4ad9d924-en.pdf?expires=1676886224&id=id&accname=ocid84004878&checksum=DAD3B788FF9D688A715466EF1D2135A7. [13]

OECD (2021), *OECD Skills Outlook 2021: Learning for Life*, OECD Publishing, Paris, https://www.oecd-ilibrary.org/docserver/0ae365b4-en.pdf?expires=1681746986&id=id&accname=ocid84004878&checksum=502647475D6197768ACBA081E248F600. [8]

OECD (2019), *Digitalisation and productivity: A story of complementarities*, OECD Economic Outlook: 2019, https://www.oecd-ilibrary.org/sites/b2e897b0-en/1/2/2/index.html?itemId=/content/publication/b2e897b0-en&_csp_=d2743ede274dd564946a04fc1f43d5dc&itemIGO=oecd&itemContentType=book. [5]

OECD (2019), *Going Digital: Shaping Policies, Improving Lives*, OECD Publishing, Paris, https://www.oecd.org/digital/going-digital-shaping-policies-improving-lives-9789264312012-en.htm. [11]

OECD (2018), *Bridging the Rural Digital Divide*, OECD Digital Economy Papers, No. No. 265, OECD Publishing, https://www.oecd-ilibrary.org/docserver/4ad9d924-en.pdf?expires=1676886224&id=id&accname=ocid84004878&checksum=DAD3B788FF9D688A715466EF1D2135A7. [14]

Portulans Institute (2020), *Focus on Taiwan and Uzbekistan*, Network Readiness Around the World, Portulans Institute, https://networkreadinessindex.org/wp-content/uploads/2020/04/Uzbeklstan.pdf. [10]

The State Committee of the Republic of Uzbekistan on Statistics (2023), *Digital Economy*, The State Committee of the Republic of Uzbekistan on Statistics, Tashkent, https://stat.uz/en/official-statistics/tsifrovaya-ekonomika-eng. [3]

The State Committee of the Republic of Uzbekistan on Statistics (2023), *Labor Market*, The State Committee of the Republic of Uzbekistan on Statistics, Tashkent, https://stat.uz/en/official-statistics/labor-market. [15]

The State Committee of the Republic of Uzbekistan on Statistics (2023), *National Accounts*, The State Committee of the Republic of Uzbekistan on Statistics, Tashkent, https://stat.uz/en/official-statistics/national-accounts. [2]

WEF (2020), *The Future of Jobs Report 2020*, WEF, Geneva, https://www.weforum.org/reports/the-future-of-jobs-report-2020. [7]

www.ingramcontent.com/pod-product-compliance
Lightning Source LLC
Chambersburg PA
CBHW061224240926
51846CB00006B/1348
9789264989733